FOOT PRINTS . . . . .

ON

THE SANDS OF TIME,

A History of . . .

    South-western Virginia

    and

North-western North Carolina.

By

DR. A. B COX.

The Star Pub. Co. Print, Sparta, N. C.,
Aug. 1900.

FOOT PRINTS ....
ON THE SANDS OF TIME,
A History of ...
South-western Virginia
and
North-western North Carolina

by
Dr. A. B. Cox

Originally Published by
The Star Publishing Company
Sparta, North Carolina
in 1900.

This edition
Copyright ©2023
Imaging Specialists. Inc.
ISBN 979-8-9861568-0-4

All rights reserved. No part of this book may be reproduced in any form or by electronic or mechanical means, including information page and retrieval systems, without permission in writing from the publisher, except by a reviewer, who may quote brief passages in a review.

First printing, February 2023

Imaging Specialists, Inc. ★ Sparta, North Carolina
WWW.STARROUTEBOOKS.COM

INDEX TO CONTENTS.

	PAGES
How this Country was Settled	11-27

SOUTH-WESTERN VIRGINIA.

Montgomery, Pulaski, Wythe, Smith	27–31
Carroll	31–40
Floyd	40–50
Grayson	50–76

NORTH-WESTERN NORTH CAROLINA.

Alleghany	76–104
Ashe	104–131
Surry	131–136
Watauga	136–148
Battle of King's Mountain	148–151
Dr. Aras. B. Cox and Family	151–162

Thank you for purchasing this edition of *Foot Prints on the Sands of Time*, by Dr. A. B. Cox.

Aras Bishop Cox was born January 25, 1816, in Floyd County, Virginia. He married Phebe Edwards, daughter of David Edwards and Jane Osborne Reeves Edwards, of Stratford, NC.

Aras Cox worked as a Methodist Clergyman in 1850. At that time, he and Phebe and their children, Mary Jane, Henry, and Edward, lived in Ashe County, NC (which at that time included the area would become Alleghany County, NC.)

By 1860, Aras had become a doctor and their family had grown to include another son, Charles.

May 3, 1862, at age 46, he enlisted in the Confederate Army in the 61st NC Infantry, where he served as Captain of Company I. He resigned that December, due to illness and disability.

In 1876 the family (Aras, Phebe, Edward, Charles, Jane, Albert, and James) lived in Atchison, Missouri.

In 1885, he and Phebe lived in Madison County, Nebraska. March 8, 1886, Dr. Cox was appointed Postmaster of Purdum, Nebraska. He was a member of the Grand Army of the Republic while he lived there.

After Phebe's death, Dr. Cox returned to Ashe County, to live with his daughter's family. At the time of the 1900 census, he lived with his son-in-law, Soloman Cox, two granddaughters, and two boarders. His daughter, Mary Jane, had passed away on August 7, 1899.

Dr. Cox passed away January 30, 1907, in Brewster, Nebraska. At the time, he was living with his son, Charles. He was buried next to his wife, in Purdum Cemetery, in Blaine County, Nebraska. A descendant states Dr. Cox donated the land for the Purdum Cemetery on the corner of his homestead.

Foot Prints on the Sands of Time was written in 1900 and originally published by Star Pub. Co. This edition uses type set by the original publishers.

While we have made an effort to correct minor technical errors, no content has been changed.

INTRODUCTION.

In the introduction of biographical and descriptive sketches of South-western Virginia and North-western North Carolina we are assured there are many incidents connected with the early settlements of the country of thrilling interest worthy a place in the records of history. The perils of life in a wild, Indian country, the hardships and toil endured by ancestors and those who sought for homes free from tyranny and oppression; from the love of liberty and justice, imbibing sentiments of self-sacrifice and heroic firmness in meeting the incidents common to border life, with forests on one side and savages on the other, shall their patriotic love of home and country and principles they cherished for the prosperity and happiness of lineal decendants and future generations be forgotten? Never! Principles cannot die; they will live and live on, to preserve a record of the discovery of America and leading events of planting colonies and extending Christian civilization over this highly favored land, and especially ancestors and pioneer settlers of the country—of which this is the special history—whose lives and labors embalmed in sacred memory that those who now or hereafter live in stately mansions or beautiful farm dwellings, adorned by beautiful shade trees, and with lawns of grass around the houses of comfort and enjoyment, the present and future generations may read with greatful appreciation the history of the lives and labors of those who, in the fear of God and love of humanity, helped to plant the tree of liberty, and nourished it with prayers and watered it with tears.

In these biographical sketches there are many who, at a more recent date, became citizens and residents who have contributed to their country's prosperity and happiness that we have not been able to record from the limits of this volume. But there are many now living in this highly favored country enjoying the blessings of home and happiness, we have especially referred to, possessing talent, statesmanship and patriotic love of home and country, under a government that administers justice to all its subjects upon whom this great nation is dependant to assist in protecting their rights, and perpetuating, sustaining and preserving in their pristine purity, the principles of government contained in the Declaration of Independence and constitution of the United States, in framing one of the best superstructures of civil government ever erected by the wisdom and genius of man. If this history perpetuates the names and records, the lives and noble deeds of ancestors and other early settlers who, through privation, hardships, toils and perseverance, have changed this great country which lay slumbering through the ages of the past from a wild, Indian, savage state to a christian civilization of intelligent, refined, enlightened population.

If we have recovered from oblivion. the name and life of any person or persons that will give comfort or cheer the living; if we have presented the lives and labors of the honored dead who left examples to the world—a richer legacy than gold or silver—to be followed to obtain the greatest blessings and sacred enjoyment of life on earth and brightest hopes of an inheritance in Heaven. If this history, however unique it may be, shall encourage somr dear boy or girl, young man or young lady to honor, comfort and rejoice the heart of a kind father and affectionate mother; if this book shall add one particle toward advancing the Redeemer's Kingdom on earth and impress the mind and heart with the obligation that is high as Heaven and lasting as Eternity which we are under to honor, love and serve God for our good and His glory,—if any of these objects are obtained we shall believe our labor not in vain. * * * We present this book to you, kind reader, as a tribute of love to our native country and the affection to its worthy people.

THE AUTHOR.

Prof. Brown's Recommendation.

We have examined some of the manuscripts prepared by Dr. A. B. Cox for a history. The work has required much labor, care and patient research and contains many things of deep interest relating to the discovery of America and early settlements of the country. and especially South-western Virginia and North western North Carolina, of which this is the history. The patriotic love of home and country free from unjust burthens of taxation and tyranny characterized the early settler of this country. Their toils, privations and hardships are carefully detailed in this work. The history gives accurate account of ancestors' lives that will be interesting to their lineal decendants, and shows the great change in the past and present condition of things. The advancement from lower to higher degrees has marked the divine economy in every department of its reign.

This history will give a statement of the lives of those who, in the past and present, have and are contributing to the good of their country. We cheerfully recommend it as a history worthy a place in every family library to perpetuate the memory of the sacred dead and worthy living who appreciate their homes in this highly favored land with an enllghtened population, institutions of learning, refined society, churches and other christian institutions that should encourage those who live afterwards to emulate the illustrious dead and in gratitude to God, the giver of every good and perfect gift, and preserve. unimpaired, the priceless heritage bequeathed us by the wisdom and genius of the founders of our civil and religious liberties.

S. W. BOWN,
Prin. Sparta Institute.

HISTORY OF

SOUTH-WESTERN VIRGINIA AND NORTH-WESTERN N. C.

History contains an important branch of science, giving accurate accounts of past events—founding governments, progress in arts and science, biographies of those who have contributed to the good of society and advancement of christian civilization. History is often a warning against error, and inspires the mind with a deep desire to be good and great, leaving on the golden pages of history an example worthy for others to imitate. The noble deeds of heroic valor and self-sacrifice for the good of others who may live afterwards, is worth the admiration of intelligent minds, calculated to inspire patriotic love of home and country and enable future generations to look with pleasing recollections on the lives of pioneer settlers who, through privation and toil paved the way from log cabins to stately mansions, halls and palaces. Historians generally record the lives of great men and eulogize their deeds. while millions in humbler walks of life perform the labor, support the government defend the rights of humanity, merit the good will and respect and honor of their country. yet their deeds are left untold.

The following pages are intended to give a brief history of South-western Virginia and North-western North Carolina and genealogical statement of the pioneer settlers and their lineal decendants, with some sketches of the discovery of this country.

South-western Virginia and North-western North Carolina are between ranges of mountains containing beautiful forests, salubrious atmosphere, crystal streams of water, rich vegetation, delicious fruits, and rich mines of iron, lead, copper and zinc. It is a subject of deep interest;— to natice the order

THE SANDS OF TIME. 13

of Divine providence that after this vast continent lay slumbering through the ages of the past, unknown to the enlightened nations of the world, waiting the magic art of the hand of civilization to cultivate its virgin soil and develop its vast resources of wealth.

Christopher Columbus, a native of the republic of Genoa, a man of superior talents, from scientific knowledge, believed there must be a continent in the West balancing the great continent in the East. After many years of toil and painful solicitations, presenting in their attractive powers the honor, wealth and fame it would confer on Spain if he could obtain an outfit to go in quest of and discover Western lands, King Ferdinand, being engaged in wars, and not being willing to risk his funds, did not favor the enterprise, but the amiable and noble Queen Isabella offered him her aid, pawning her own jewels to raise funds. Her name is worthy to be engraved in letters of gold on the records of American history. Three vessels were fitted up and, on the 3rd day of August, after repairing to the chapel and offering up prayer to Almighty God for the success of the voyage, they sailed from the port Palos in Spain, and with admirable courage, patience and skill in overcoming difficulties, on the 12th of October they discovered Hispaniola, one of the West India islands. After setting foot on its soil they knelt in prayer, thanking God for their success. They made other discoveries and returned to spain.

A second and a third voyage was made and further discoveries continued until the reign of Queen Elizabeth, which was one of the brightest and most exciting in English history.

Sir Walter Raleigh, whose name is held in grateful memory, enjoyed, at that time, the favor of the Queen and obtained letters patent from the crown and fitted up an expedition, consisting of two vessels, commanded by Phillip Armadas and Arthnr Barlow, sailed on the 27th of April, A. D. 1584, and landed on Roanoke Island on the 4th day of July of that year. They met a friendly reception from the natives The scenery was delightful. There were plenty of fine grapes and berries. The air was redolent with sweet perfume from the beautiful flowers. It was here on Currituck Sound the first Anglo-Saxon meteor flag floated to the breeze; and it was here on this newly discovered country that the silence was broken by the first christian prayer from grateful hearts that went up to God.

A kind entertainment was given to Armadas and Barlow and their men by the wife of Granganameo, an Indian chief, that would have done honor to female humane kindness among enlightened people in the most refined society. The expedition returned to England in September of the same year. During the year following, April, 1585, another expedition, consisting of over one hundred persons, under the auspices of Sir Walter Raleigh, was sent to Roanake. These returned to England after a year's absence; and still another was sent out by him in 1586, in charge of John White, commissioned as governor of the city of Roanoke, to be established on Roanoke Island. White returned to England leaving about one hundred men, women and children, among whom was his daughter, Eleanor Dare, wife of one of the assistants, and who, on the 18th of August, became mother of the first child—Virginia Dare by name—born of English parents in the New world.

It was not until the year 1590 that Raleigh could return to look after his colony. Not a trace of it could be found. After fitting out

five expeditions at his own expense—about
$200,000—and laboring many years, he abandoned his possessions, despairing of success.
His ignominious judicial murder by a government he had patriotically devoted the best energies of his great mind and life, must, for all
time to come, stand out conspicuousy on the
dark pages of her high crimes

For a half century no successful efforts
were made to establish colonies in North Carolina. Mean while other settlements were
being made in Virginia. It was here where
so great an effort was made and so great a
sacrifice of life and treasure to establish a
colony that the principles of liberty. justice
and right were rocked in the cradle of freedom, and the foundation of a great Anglo-American Empire laid, the principles of human government simplified, the liberty of the
people and their right to self government immovably established. A free, happy and
powerful republic under the constitution of
laws in which the rights of individuals are as
inviolably sustained as the glory of the national faith that now covers the fairest portion of
the new world. The proudest result of this
new born nation is the purity of its government and the happiness of its people. She

THE SANDS OF TIME.

has given to the world the sublime lesson of her experience and great principles of free government.

We now return to the more permanent settlement made in North Carolina. It was more than fifty years after the loss of the colony left by White on Roanoke before any permanent settlement was made in North Carolina. A colony had been settled in Virginia about 1620 and—during and thereafter—up to 1640 colonists from Virginia united with emigrants from other counties in making a more permanent settlement in North Carolina. From dissention and divisions among the settlers and trouble with the Indians great care and perseverance was required to retain peace, order and safety. Christian fortitude added much in crowning success.

A colony was commenced in Virginia A. D. 1608 under the wise counsel and leadership of Captain Jonh Smith whose life and past experience prepared him for the important work entrusted to his care. While engaged in this arduous task an incident occurred worthy of record. Captain Smith was taken prisoner by the Indians and sentence of death passed upon him by Powhatan, a ruling Indian Chief. Preparation was made for his execution; His head lay on a rock, the savage executioner's war-club raised to strike the fatal blow when Pocahontas, the eldest daughter of Chief Powhatan, laid her head on Smith's declaring she would peril her own life to save his. Such acts of female sympathy, love and humane kindness from his (the Chief's) own daughter touched the savage Chief's heart and he changed his sentence saying, his life should not be taken. Smith was set at liberty and powatan became the friend of the English and did much for the success of the colony. The gallant deed prompted by love that glowed in the heart of the Indian maid, so beautifully manifested by Pocahontas in periling her own life to save another, is worthy the praise of the brightest intellect under Christian culture. Pocahontas was carried to England, married to John Rolfe, a worthy young Englishman, professed the Christian religion, was baptised under the name of Rebecca and died an example of peaceful resignation and buried at Gravesend in England. From her lineal decendants sprang some of the leading families as scholars and statesmen. Captain Smith, exercising great administrative ability in governing the class of emigrants that first came to Virginia and de-

THE SANDS OF TIME. 19

fending his people from Indian depradations, succeeded in planting a colony permanently in Virginia. During the year 1620, after much toil, privation and suffering his valuable life was closed in England.

We have given an account of that part of Captain Smith's life in Virginia and circumstances attending it believing it would be of interest to the reader. His rescue by Pocahontas was an act of such love and heroism by a youthful maid—daughter of a savage chief—that would have done honor to the brightest female intellect in an enlightened land of Christian civilization, exciting the strongest principles of charity and Christian culture— the deeds of such sainted women as Ruth and Mary and Mary Magdalene who loved Jesus, and other noble women whose names will live engraven on the pages of infinite memory when marble monuments will have crumbled into dust—should be retained in history as jewels of woman's love and power.

When the first English settlement was made they became restless, and there being no women in the colony the English were not satisfied. In the fall of 1820 ninety young women were induced to cast their fortunes and seek husbands in Virginia, and soon after sixty others— courageous marriageable women— landed in the new settlement and became wives to the pioneers. The ladies were sold to the colonists who were allowed to make their selection and to pay their passage to the London company

The population increased and settlements continued westward. In 1635 the London company sent over Sir John Harvey to govern the colony, but he conducted things so badly that the patience of the people gave way and Harvey was sent back to England a prisoner to answer for his misconduct The English law of primogeniture and detail regula- the descent of property, and the wealthier colonists, directing the labor of many indented servants and slaves who lived apart on their plantations, affecting somewhat of a landed aristocracy. After the ruination of the King's cause at home in 1645 many of the disbanded cavaliers found refuge in Virginia, bringing with them chivalrous attachments of church and king.

In 1671 Governor Berkley estimated the population at 40,000 —including 2,000 negro slaves and 6,000 indented servants. The character of his administration may be inferred from a communication made by him this year to the English privy council: "I thank God there are no free schools here or printing press and I hope will not be for the next hundred years, for education only makes subjects disloyal to the King." The spirit of liberty and justice grew with increase of population. A young lawyer by the name of Bacon came to the colony but soon raised a disturbance and was arrested by order of Berkley and he and his followers severely punished. Berkley afterwards returned to England. He was not received with applause, but rather, it is said, with chagrin.

The colony still extended its territory westward. It was during Sir George Yeadly's administration as Governor of the colony of Virginia that the territory was divided into eleven districts or boroughs. The Governor issued a proclamation to the citizens of each borough to elect two of their own number to constitute a legislative assembly. Elections were accordingly held on the 30th of July, 1619. The delegates convened at Jamestown. Here was organized the Virginia house of Burgeses or colonial legislature—the first popular assembly held in the new world. Here was laid the first piller for a great republic. A few years after the plantation of Jamestown other settlements were made up the James river as far as Richmond and beyond. The commonwealth of Virginia grew and expanded according to national laws of development. Emigrants came in from Ireland, Scotland, Germany and other European countries; the natives mulitipied; others came to find new homes in this favored land, society improved, civil and religious institutions established to meet the wants of the colony.

The permanence of a new state was assured. This country became a place of refuge from religious persecution and heavy burdens of taxation. For near one hundred years the people contended, not only with hardships incident to pioneer life, but almost continual Indian warfare, until the 17th century. The love of liberty and the administration of justice had taken hold on the minds of the people, not to be erased, and patriotic love of home and country planted in virtuous soil to live and expand to other lands. At the beginning of the 17th century the colony had advanced in Virginia as far west as Montgomery county, which at that time included a considerable part of South-western Virginia.

Believing it will be a matter of pleasing interest to the lineal decendants of ancestors who left their native homes in the densely populated and down-trodden countries of the old world, and came to this country, and through indefatigable labor and toil aided in unfurling the banner of liberty and religious freedom which they happily enjoyed. We give a statement of some of the leading families that first settled in this country and some of the incidents therewith—partly from tradition and the most reliable sources of information we could obtain The Craigs, Englishes, Lewises, Triggs, Taylors, Huffs, Coxes, Cloyds, Prestons, Floyds, Charletons. Wades, Howards, Lesters and Dobbins. These families by united effort, established permanent homes, and their lineal descendants are scattered over this broad land, west to the Pacific coast.

Towns and cities have been built up, railroads completed, navigation enlarged, institutions of learning established, inventions that have equaled if not surpassed the genius of any others that the world has ever produced. Fulton, the inventor of the steam boat, Fields of the ocean cable, Whitney, of the cotton gin, and Edison of the telephone. The families mentioned have borne a conspicuous part in founding the institutions so happily enjoyed by the people of the present generation.

John Craige, of Roanoke, married Mollie Cox, whose son represented his district in congress for many years. Craige county was named in honor of his family. James Taylor, a nephew of the representative in congress, was for some years Attorney-General of Virginia. The Preston family was distinguished for their patriotism and love of country. General James Preston was wounded in the war of 1812 and made a cripple for life, and afterwards became Governor of Virginia. His son Hon. Wm. B. Preston was an able statesman and distinguished lawyer, was Secretary of the Navy in Pres. William Henry Harrison's cabinet, and with ex-President Tyler, as a delegate from Virginia to the peace congress which convened at Washington City to prevent the unfortunate war between the states. Gordon Cloyd lived in Pulaski county and was Entry-taker in the land office for many years. Captain John Cox, brother of Mrs. Craige referred to, was at one time a citizen of Montgomery county, moved to Grayson county. Virginia, was distinguished as a Regulator during the Revolutionary war. The Lesters were noted for energy and ambition in whatever they engaged in, always honest and right.

Peter Howard, the ancestor of the Howard family, was a worthy Baptist minister. He lived to a good old age, raised an intelligent family. Col. Joseph Howard was one of the country's best citizens, honored and respected by the people. Rev. Charles W. Charleton, of Montgomery county, was a talented, interesting preacher, member of Holston annual conference of the M. E. Church South for some years. The original ancestors of the Bishop family came from Holland. They were among the first settlers of Floyd, then Montgomery county. The old lady was drowned in Little river in an attempt to cross when it was too flush. Henry and Jacob, their sons, were large athletic men, noted for industry and prudence in managing the business affairs of life. The Andersons and Wades were quiet, reliable families, often filling county offices. A Mr. Wade is the present Clerk of Montgomery county. Roanoke retains the name of Roanoke given to the island at the mouth of the Roanoke river, at which point Armadas and Barlow landed in

1584. It is a beautiful city with an intelligent and enterprising population, large manufactories and wholesale inecrantile stores. The surrounding country is rich in mineral wealth and fine farms. They have fine public buildings, churches and institutions of learning.

CHAPTER II.

Montgomery county has many things of historic nature connected with it. It is situated just west of the range of Alleghanies and divides the eastern and western waters. Christiansburg is the capital. The Norfolk and Western railroad passes through its centre. It contains fine farm and grazing lands. Its society is refined.

Pulaski county is noted for its production of grain and grasses. Newburn is the capital. In this county several prominent families reside. Floyds, Wysors, Drapers, Cloyds and Wygals, some of whom filled important offices.

The county of Wythe is rich in mineral wealth; iron, lead, gypsum, cobalt and zinc. Iron furnaces, manufactories and public works have given employment to many laboring hands. The distinguished General Samuel Houston, the hero of Sanjacinto, first president of the republic of Texas, was born at the lead mines, in Wythe county. Judge Andrew Fulton resided in this county and was a representative in Congress, but was a native of North Carolina, which State was proud of her son. Colonel Rush Floyd was a talented lawyer and at the head of the bar. Pierce owned residences, furnaces manufactories of shot and other extensive business operations, and was at Poplar Camp. in the southeastern part of the county. Many Germans and Dutch were early settlers of this county and formed a class of the finest agriculturalists in the country. Wytheville, the capital, is a beautiful town and an active place of business, and has a fine institution of learning conducted under the wise administration of Prof. Snavely. The adaptation of grain-growing, stock-raising, mineral wealth, and commercial advantages make the county of Wythe one of the most desirable places for a pleasant home.

Smith county, although not large in boundary, contains much wealth. It has a rich alluvial soil, fine timber, and furnishes much mateaial for buildings. Its minerals are salt, and gypsum. Marion, the county seat, is delightfully located, and is laid out in beauty and convenience and is a desirable place for a happy home, where refined society churches and good schools and fine railroad facilities are to be found. The salt works in the Southwestern part of the county has furnished millions of bushels to the surrounding country. These connties of Virginia produce fine fruits, such as apples, peaches, pears. quinces and abundance of smaller fruits. Look & Lincoln manufacture valuable articles for wagons, etc., that supply the pressing demands of the country. The Seven Mile Ford farm is very beautiful—level, rich soil, crystal streams of Holston river— and rich in production equal to any on the Mississippi river. James W. Sheffey was a resident of this county and was an able jurist. James White Sheffey and George W. Richardson are practicing lawyers of Marion. The lunatic asylum is located near town and is an honor to christian civilization. The officers of this institution—Dr. Preston, Superintendent—are gentlemen eminently qualified for the important duties assigned them. Major Scott was for many years Sheriff of Smyth county and proved a faithful offi cer and honored citizen. His was a noble family. Their son, Robert D. Scott, is editor of the Enterprise Battle Creek, Nebraska. Miss Mattie Scott was a lady of refinement and many accomplishments.

CHAPTER III.

SOUTH-WESTERN VIRGINIA.

Carroll County.

There is much of historic lore attached to South-western Virginia. The genealogy of Carroll and surrounding counties is so immediately connected that anything like a correct chronology cannot be given without taking the population in connection.

Carroll county is bounded on the east by Floyd, on the south by Surry, N. C., (State line), on the west by Grayson, on the North by Wythe.

Hillsville is the county seat. This town is a neat country village with well-arranged streets for convenience in business departments, and is well supplied with hotels, mercantile establishments, doctors, lawyers and merchants. The Elliott House is a good hotel for the weary traveler. It has all the accommodations that polite attention and kindness can bestow. Mr. Thompson, the gentlemanly proprietor gives his guests a pleasant home at his hotel.

Carroll county abounds in fine meadow and grazing lands, forests of fine timber, beautiful streams of cool, clear, soft water which passes through most all the farm land. Iron, in large quantities, zinc and copper abound. The productions are wheat, rye, oats, corn and buckwheat.

This county claims to have derived its name from Charles Carroll, one of the signers of the Declaration of Independence. John Blair was one of the early settlers who owned and operated iron works on Chestnut Creek and supplied the people with a much needed article. He represented his county in the legislature before Carroll county was formed from the eastern end of Grayson county. His wife was a Miss Boring They raised an intelligent family. Hon. Fielding J. Hale, of Battle Creek, Nebraska, is a lineal descendant of the Blair family. Many of their posterity are scattered through the western states. Andrew Cock was among the first set-

tlers of the eastern part of the county. He
made and occupied a fine farm on Burk's Fork
of Reed Island river. One of his daughters,
Hannah, is the grandmother of Rev. Mr.
Webb, of the county. After the death of this
venerable pioneer his son, Esquire John Cock,
became owner of the old homestead. His
wife was Jennie Phillips, one of earth's noble
women. Esquire Cock served his county as
Justice of the Peace for many years. He was
an upright man and leader in his community.
Their large family decendants have, many of
them, gone West to occupy new territory.
Reuben Cock was also an early settler and
raised a large respected family. The population of the eastern part of Carroll county was
composed in part of Daltons, Bobbitts, Nestors, Jenkinses, Webbs and Montgomeries.
John Carroll (Irish descent) was a merchant,
farmer and representative in the legislature.
John Cock, Jr., married his neice, Mary Ann
Carroll; William Bobbitt married her sister,
Margaret Carroll. Jeremiah Star was a
worthy citizen and successful farmer and
tanner. His wife was Tabitha Howell, granddaughter of Enoch Orsborn, Sr., of Bridle
Creek, Grayson county. Louis, Wesly and

Mary were their children. Captain Jennings who commanded a company from the eastern part of the county in the Confederate army, was a young man of talents and much moral worth who fell in battle an honor to his extensive family relations and country, as was also the brave company under his command. William Lindsey, first Clerk of the court, and Robert Mitchell were prominent citizens and Justices of the Peace. Col. Madison D. Carter, lawyer and farmer, resided in this part of the county and earnestly labored for the good of his country. He was an honored and respected citizen

Edward Marshall was Sheriff for a num- of years, an efficient, faithful officer. Wm. Kenny was a practical farmer and a worthy citizen and had a highly respected family. Dr. Joshua D. Stoneman had an extensive practice in this and adjoining counties. He was a zealous member of the Quaker church, loved, honored and respected. His son, Mark D. Stoneman, made medicine his profession and moved to Indiana. The Davis families were quiet, good citizens. Esquire Coolie lived in the western part of the county. No modern Tubal Cain could have excelled him as an artificer in his superior skill in working metals. He made some of the finest clocks in the United States. One of these clocks were purchased by John McMillan, of Alleghany county, and it not only kept the usual order of time, but the days of the week and the month, the "full" and changes of the moon. The author of these sketches has often seen the clock. Esquire Coolie was a useful and honored citizen and had an intelligent and highly respected family.

Rev. William Thompson, a native of Campbell county, Va., for some time a resident of Floyd county, spent the close of his useful life near Hillsville after having served his generation by the will of God. His happy spirit no doubt has gone to gather laurels fresh that will never fade in the regions of bliss.

There are many worthy subjects connected with the people we have not recorded; their lives and noble deeds are worthy of being perpetuated. Rev. Vaughn and Amos Shockley were local preachers in the M. E. Church South who aided in unfurling the banner of the cross over their people. They have gone to rest in the better world but the fruits of their labor still live.

Elder William Lawson, a distinguished

distinguished lawyer and statesman, presidential elector and member of congress. His wife, Miss Pannel, possessed a high order of talent and christian culture as governess in the family circle, both as teacher in literature and christian education that does honor to the name of mother. Their son, General James E. B. Stewart, commanded a brigade of cavalry in the Confederate army, was wounded at Yellow Tave, Va , and died a meritorious officer of whom his county and state is justly proud.

Many worthy families live in Patrick county, some of whom we name, as Staples, Penns. Reeds, Scales, Moores and Cores, all have done credit to their county and state. Rev Jacob Bishop resided in this county for more than forty years was a quiet local preacher in the M. E. Church South for nearly sixty years. A fine church edifice was erected in his neighborhood, known as Gladeville church, with a membership of over one hundred. Wm. Liddle, was a class-leader. Rev. Alexander C. Sutherland and Rev. Ezra Painter were local preachers.

Chestnut Yards, in the western part of the county, is the terminus of a branch of the Norfolk & Western railroad. Wolf Glade, six miles east of old Grayson courthouse on turnpike road leading to Hillsville, is an active place of business, having dry goods and grocery stores, fine steel roller flour mills and a tannery in a wealthy community of good farmers and successful producers. Of the worthy number are Messrs. Draper, manufacturer of leather; William Liddell, a native of England, a skillful workman in iron and steel; William R. Bishop, a practical farmer and live stock dealer. His amiable accomplished wife was Miss Ella Lauson, daughter of Elder William Lauson previously mentioned. Luther Bishop, farmer and live stock dealer. His wife was a Miss Cecil, an excellent lady. Rev. A. C. Sutherland, a good farmer and producer. His accomplished wife was the daughter of Michael Kinser. Mr. Sutherland's son, Rev. Roby Sutherland, is a member of the Holston annual conference, stationed at Bristol. Although a young man in age he is distinguished as an able minister of the gospel. Dr Dobbins is located at wolf Glade, and is a successful practitioner. His wife was Miss Ella Duffy, daughter of Dr. Duffy, of Oldtown, in Grayson county Dr. Dobbins is a young man whose devotion to his profession, assisted by his excellent christian wife, bespeaks

THE SANDS OF TIME. 39

for them a bright future. James Wilkinson resides at Hillsville, and is an active business man, farmer, producer and live stock dealer. His worthy wife was Miss Jane Reeves, of Alleghany county, N. C., an excellent lady and pious companion. Steven Wilkinson, now residing at Hillsville, has been an explorer to some considerable extent, has visited Congo Free State, in Africa and Klondike regions among the gold mines of Alaska. His estimable wife was a Miss Edwards, of Wilkes county, N. C.

There is something in store for the future of Carroll county that may soon be developed. Its rich mineral deposits, fine forests of timber, granite, water power, variety of fruits, salubrious air and crystal springs of pure water are the natural blessings which are sure to prove advantageous to the people May the good people be thankful for the past and cherish bright hopes for the future.

CHAPTER IV.

SOUTH-WESTERN VIRGINIA.

Floyd County.

Floyd county was formed from the Southern part of Montgomery county. It is bounded on the south by Patrick, west by Carroll, east by Franklin. Its surface is very uneaven, All parts of the county abound in springs of clear, cold, soft water, with inlets and creeks in great numbers passing through the county. Jacksonville is the capital and is beautifully located. The population is composed of intelligent, active and enterprising business. people. Institutions of learning, supplied with well qualified professors of literature.

The Buffalo mountain in the southern part of the county rises in sublime grandeur

THE SANDS OF TIME. 41

and clouds float along its sides, and flashes of lightning and peals of thunder are seen and heard below its summit. A fine view of the surrounding country can be obtained from the top of this mountain.

The products of the county are wheat, corn, rye, oats, buckwheat, potatoes, and a great variety of vegetables and fine delicious fruits. The climate and soil is adapted to the growth of grasses, such as timothy, clover, red top and blue grass. Live stock raising has brought more money to the county than any other branch of business. There are valuable minerals. For many years past furnaces have been operated. Even gold has been found in the north-eastern part of the county. There is an alum cave in the western part of the county, also a very fine chalibeate sulphur spring. Fine forests of timber abound. Granite and sandstone, for building material, is plentiful. It has water power for mills and machinery. And there is room and power for more machinery.

The author of these sketches is a native of Floyd county; bound by endearing ties of kindre love and friendly associations of past years. We gratefully appreciate the enjoyment of the home and associations of early life. The recollection on memory's page is a green spot and cooling shade on life's journey.

Believing it will be a subject of interest and pleasure to those who now or hereafter may live to find recorded in history the names of ancient and worthy citizens who made their homes in this country worthy of a record in history, leaving examples of moral excellence and piety that enables them to look back with grateful hearts that in the providence of God they had such fine parents whose names still live in history, and whose labors changed the wild forest to fertile fields, and savage tents to happy dwelling houses, mansions, palaces, institutions of learning and churches dedicated to the worship of God.

Edmund Vansel was one of the first settlers of this county. He was a live stock raiser and good farmer. His fine farm was afterwards owned by Col. John English, Samuel Sanders and Judge Flemming Sanders. It is now owned by Mr. Burnett. The early settlers of this county were to some extent made up of emigrants from England, Germany, Ireland, Scotland and France. We give the names of some of the leading families: Phlegers, Weddles, Harmons, Slushers, Bishops, Coxes, Hiltons, Reeds, Gordons,

Wades, Helms, Howards, Goodykoontzes, Kitermans, Phillipses, Dickersons, Thurmans, Duncans, Lesters, Simmonses and Shelors. Many worthy people who made homes in this county furnished examples of industry, patience, energy and perseverance that honor head and heart.

Col Jacob Helms married a Miss Smith He was a successful merchant, farmer and active business man, a member of the Virginia legislature, when Montgomery and Floyd were one county, and, zealously aided by Hon. William B. Preston, State senator, Floyd county was created As a citizen, was a public-spirited man who contributed to the good of society. The home of Col. Helms was a preaching place for the Methodist itinerant preacher on that circuit, and a hospitalable home for way-worn ministers of the gospel. Col. Helms and family contribted much towards the ererction of a campmeeting location near their home. Captain John W. Helms was a practical farmer on Burke's Fork in the western part of the county and was Sheriff of his county for a number of years and representative of Floyd county in the Virginia legislature. He married Miss Susan Cox, a native of the

the county   Their youngest son, George W. Helms, is the present superintendent of the Virginia penitentiary and is an efficient and approved official. Wm. Goodson was first clerk of Floyd county, Pleasant Howell was sheriff and representative in the legislature, William Gilham was a representative in the legislature, Harvey Deskins was a merchant and representative, Burdine Bishop was a representative in 1883 and '84, David Slusher has been sheriff several years, Brame Bros. are editors of the Floyd Press, Mrs. Mary L. Bishop, former editor of Floyd Press, is a lady of intelligence and refinement.

The directory of Jacksonville as taken in the fall of 1895, shows seven stores, three hotels, ten lawyers four doctors, two resident ministers, one academy and two good county schools, Dr. Pendleton. druggist; S. W. Tompkins, post master; J. W. Simmons, M. D., and Calahan Stigleman, M. D., resident physicians.

We name a few of the moldel agriculturists and producers of the county : Benjamin Dodd owned a good farm one mile east of the court house, was an industrious and worthy citizen. Solomon Harmon was a farmer and miller who, by industry and economy, made a handsome property sufficient to leave his fami-

Baptist minister, who resided in the northwestern part of Patrick county. He married a Miss Thompson, an amiable christian lady. He was pastor of several churches in Carroll and adjoining counties. His superior talents and bright intellect, although limited in opportunity for education in early life, was well cultivated for usefulness in church and State He was a systematic farmer, a prudent manager of the domestic business of life, that makes the family circle a happy home, worth living for. The writer that records these facts, has, when wearied by traveling, spent several nights' rest with this hospitable family. Elder Lawson continued faithful in his ministerial work as long as he was able to travel. "He, being dead, yet speaketh " He has gone to his happy home to dwell with the church triumphant in glory. Their son, Col. Jefferson Lawson, was an officer in the Confederate army, honored and respected, after the war, representative in the Legislature.

The population of Patrick county is so immediately connected with that of Carroll in relations of life that they may be appropriately described together. Hon. Archibald Stuart, of Patrick county, practiced law in Carroll courts for several years. He was a

ly in good circumstances. Andrew Weddle
was an unassuming christian whose wife was
a Miss Boone, a relative of the celebrated
Daniel Boone, of Kentucky renown. Mr. Weddle was a pattern of industry, quietude and
piety. Archibald Hylton was an excellent
citizen and practical farmer. Ambrose Cox,
Sr., lived in the western part of the county
married Miss Sallie Reed. He was a good
citizen and neighbor and by industry and
economy acquired considerable wealth. His
father Matthew Cox senior was a native of the
valley of Virginia. His wife's maiden name
was Dickenson, who first married a man by
the name of Spencer. She was a widow when
Matthew Cox married her. Their union was
blessed with six sons and one daughter, viz:
Carter, Maston, Aras, Matthew, Ambrose,
Braxton and Delphine. The latter married
William Roberts. Matthew Cox, Sr , was a
soldier in Col. George Washington's regiment with General Braddoc at Pittsburg in
1755 when the English were defeated. Col.
Washington requested General Braddock to
allow him to take his regiment and fight the
indians, assuring him that under proper
discipline he could defeat them. But the
General replied: "It is high time when a

Virginia Buckskin attempts to advise a British General." The French and Indians poured a deadly fire into the English ranks until General Braddock was mortally wounded, and exclaimed: "Colonel Washington, what shall we do?" Washington answered: "For God's sake retreat!', Matthew Cox was with the body-guard that conveyed the wounded General from the fatal battle-ground. He died soon after. The Virginia regiment came near starving before they reached the valley of Virginia. Matthew Cox and family lived for some years in Halifax county, Virginia, and then moved to Floyd county, as previously stated, then moved to Wilkes county, N. C., now Caldwell county.

Esquire Isbel in after years owned the farm where Matthew Cox, Sr., lived, and where he and his noble wife's bodies rest in their honored graves. Spring Camp farm, at the foot of Buffalo mountain, on the south side, is one of the most valuable farms in the county. It was owned by Hon. Charles C. Lee, a distinguished lawyer and statesman, whose patriotic love of country reflected credit on himself and country. This valuable farm was afterward owned by Nat Burwell and brothers.

Laurel Fork, a branch of Big Reed Island, contains fine meadows and grazing lands. The old Stanly farm on Burk's Fork, north side of Buffalo mountain, contains one of the finest meadows in all this country. This farm was afterward owned by the Hylton Family. On this delightful stream was the residence of the late John W. Helms, spoken of. The Indian Ridge in the western part of the county contained some fine specimens of beautiful silica, one alone weighed twenty-five pounds, of rare beauty and was placed in the cabinet of minerals at Marion Sims college of medicine at St. Louis, Mo., with proper engravings in letters of gold, in memory of Albert S. A. Cox, a student of the college, who died there in 1891, a bright example of moral excellence anp piety. This extraordinary specimen was found by Mr. Weeks and purchased by Thomas W. Williamson, and purchased from Mr. Williamson by Dr. A. B. Cox who placed it in the college as an evidence of a father's love to his son, whose piety, bright intellect. desire for knoweledge and love of home and family did honor to his home and parents.

Elder Jesse Jones was a minister of the gospel in the Baptist church for more than sixty years. He was loved and respected as a faithful good man, the fruits of whose labor will live and live on for years to come, while he is receiving a rich reward for his faithful ministerial labor. William Smith, in the (Dunkard) German Baptist church, was one of the early preachers of Floyd county. He built up an extensive church and was truly a good and successful preacher. It is a source of pleasing recollection and grateful appreciation to the author of these sketches to remember the large number of Methodist preachers, local and itinerant, who labored so faithfully for the good of society and advancement of the Redeemer's cause on earth—the salvation of souls and glory of God. We are glad to record the names of the servants of the blessed Redeemer who obeyed the command: "Go thou and preach the kingdom of God." John Cecil, George Godby, Henry Bishop, Alfred Goodykoontz, David Howell, Jacob Bishop, Elias Skelton, Richard Buckingham and William Thompson who labored faithfully to build up the Master's kingdom of righteousness on earth, and as instruments in the church of Christ, saved souls. Among the faithful servants in the Master's vineyard none probably did more for the cause of christianity than Rev. William Thompson, especially in Methodist doctrine and discipline. His life, with the others mentioned, will live embalmed in sacred memory. There are many worthy people of Floyd county whose names are entitled to a record in commemoration of their valuable lives, but it is impossible to insert it all herein. One other we will refer to is known as old uncle Blanch Duncan, a natural genius in wood-work, and iron; a carpenter, mill-wright and blacksmith; a good neighbor and worthy citizen, who lived on Indian creek.

CHAPTER V.

SOUTH-WESTERN VIRGINIA.

GRAYSON COUNTY.

Grayson county contains the south-western corner of Virginia. The Iron mountain on the north, Stone mountain on the west, Blue Ridge on the south form its boundary. White Top, Balsam and Pond mountains clustering together at the north-west corner of the county make a valley of rich alluvial soil. The county contains forests of fine timber, crystal streams of clear, cold water. It produces fine crops of wheat, rye, oats, corn and buckwheat, and vegetables of great variety.

The county is divided into two valleys by Buck mountain. The valley of New River is on the south side and Elk Creek valley on the

North side. The advantages possessed in this locality for good homes attracted the attention of early immigrants who sought a place of residence in this (Eldorado) new territory.

The following are the names of some of the leading families that settled at an early date and made their early homes in Grayson county: Orsbornes, Coxes, Reeveses, Hashes, Phippses, Wards, Hales, Tultons, Ferrells, Borings, Thomases and Perkinses, whose lineal decendants have in some degree gone to help populate almost every state west of the Pacific coast.

Esquire Enoch Orsborn and family settled on New River, in what is known as Bridle Creek, but for many years known as Orsborn settlement. About the same time other families located there. Enoch Orsborn had three brothers, Solomon, Ephraim and Jonathan, who came to the county with their families about the same time.

A fort was built on the farm now occupied and owned by Joshua Orsborne and son, John, at Ansella post office. Indian depradations were common on the border settlements, and preparations for protection and defense was necessary. It was fortunate for society that the first settlers were people of moral worth and piety.

Enoch Orsborne and wife were professors of religion and aided in planting the standard of christian civilization over the land that was recently inhabited by savages. An incident occurred with the Osborne brothers in their newly occupied territory that tells of the dangers and exposures to which pioneer settlers were subjected. Enoch Orsborn and brothers, Solomom and Ephraim, went into what is now Wautauga, N. C., on a hunting trip—deer being plentiful in that section—and getting wet by a shower of rain and wet bushes struck up camp, hung up their wet clothes by the camp-fire and lay down to sleep. The Indians surprised them by shooting and killing Solomon Orsborn. An Indian chased Enoch some distance and lost him in the dark. Ephraim, after fleeing from camp, carefully crept back in the dark to his mare that was fastened with a hickory-bark halter to a tree, loosed her and rode home. Enoch Orsborne returned home without shoes and in his night clothing. The author of these sketches learned these facts from Mrs. Mary McMuller who, before her marriage, was Miss Mary Woods, granddaughter of Solomon Orsborn who was murdered by the Indians, and married Hon. Fayette McMuller, member of congress from Scott county in his district in Virginia for several sessions. It was at the old fort where Esquire Enoch Orsborn, Sr., first located a home. He married a Miss Hash. Their home was a resting place for the way-worn traveling preachers. The venerable Bishop Ashbury, in after years called with them, rested and took refreshments as he was making his ministerial tour through this newly settled country, preaching the gospel.

Captain John Cox and his brother, David, moved to Grayson county and settled on New River about ten miles west of Grayson old Court House. John Cox was captain of the Regulators of this part of the state during the Rovolutionary war and, as far as he could, kept peace and prevented crime. In after years he moved to the mouth of Cranberry Creek, Ashe county, N. C., south fork of New River, made and cultivated a large farm and raised live stock, and where, when life's arduous toils were over, was buried in the family graveyard. His body rests in peace. His old residence is owned in part by Ellis McNeill at this time. They had two sons,

James and Joshua. James Cox married widow Terrell, Joshua Cox married a Miss Richardson. Their daughters married as follows: Catherine married Henry Harden, Cynthia married William Gambill, Jane married Canada Richardson, another daughter (name unknown) married Thomas McGimpsy, and snother daughter (name unknown) married a Mr. Baker.

David Cox, brother of Captain John Cox, moved his family to Grayson county and located their home in the same neighborhood where his brother, Captain John Cox stopped for several years—on New River, ten or twelve miles west of Grayson old Court House. David Cox's wife was a Miss McGowan They had seven sons and three daughters, whose lives were directly connected with other good citizens in laboring for the interest of the county in all that pertained to success, prosperity and future happiness.

George Reeves and family settled in the same neighborhood. They came from eastern Virginia. Mr. Reeves' wife's maiden name was Burton. She was a pious Christian woman whose counsel and example still lives. They had four sons and four daughters who met the responsibilities of their day with energy and success. Benjamin Phipps came from Rowan county, N. C., settled on Bridle Creek. His brother, Isaiah came about the same time, as did also the Hash family. Benjamin Phipps married Miss Jane Hash, an excellent good woman She lived to be near one hundred years old; lived to see her children and grandchildren to the fourth generation.

William Boring and family were early settlers who built the first iron works in the county. The place is known as the old furnace on Rock Creek now owned by Joshua Cox. Mr, Boring was clerk of the county for a number of years. Their daughter, Mary married Col. Martin Dickenson who resided at Old Town, was county clerk and hotel keeper. Their son, William Boring, Jr., was a worthy citizen. He and his excellent wife raised a family that did honor to their parents and country. Their daughter, Miss Lucinda married Freelin Nuckolls who moved to Chyenne, Wyoming Territory, and was the first representative of the Territory in congress. Richard Hale settled on Elk Creek with his brothers, William, Frank, Dudley, Louis, Stephen and John. William Hale married a Miss Stone. Stephen and Louis married each a Miss Boring. Frank and Dudley married each a Miss Burrus. John married a Miss Blair. These were industrious, persevering citizens and helped materially to advance the best interests of Grayson county We refer to some of their descendants futher over.

Andrew Hampton and his brother, Wade Hampton came over from England and settled near Lexington, N. C. Andrew Hampton, Jr., married Miss Sallie Mima. Their son, Griggs Hampton married Miss Phillis Sutherland. They raised nine sons and five daughters. Mr. Hampton's nice farm is a few miles west of Grayson Old Town, where he and his family enjoyed a happy home. It is a beautiful homestead. Their son, Litle H. Hampton who lives near there, is a practical farmer and fruit grower. His excellent wife was Miss Nancy Blevins, grandaughter of Esquire Samuel and Rebecca Cox. Hemper Hampton married Miss Anna Nuckolls and resided in the county. He was a good farmer and business man and raised an industrious worthy family.

John Clemens—whose wife was a Miss Nuckolls—lived at Grayson Old Court House.

He kept a hotel. Their sons were Frank, Logan and John, their daughter, Jule. John went to Nebraska and was the first person buried in the cemetery at Nebraska City.

Amos Ballard and family lived at Grayson Old Court House. The old gentleman's business was to "cry sales"—an auctioneer—but laughed most of the time, or rather made others laugh while he was crying.

Major Anderson—whose wife was a Miss Nuckolls—resided in the county. He was a prominent citizen of Grayson county. Their sons were Robert, Orville and Garland. Robert and family moved to Atchison County, Mo. They were pious members of the M. E. church South and rendered efficient assistance in building the first church edifice for the M. E. church South in the county. Major Orville Anderson was one of the best clerks in south-western Virginia. His bright intellect, devoted christian life, and example still live. Garland Anderson was a quiet good citizen.

Samuel Fulton and family lived on Elk Creek. He served his people as Justice of the Peace for many years. Their son, Rev. Creed Fulton was a minister of the gospel in the M. E. church South—a distinguished pulpit orator—and a zealous successful friend of education. It was in greater part through his agency that Emory & Henry college was established. The college is a monument of what faith, patience, energy and perseverance will accomplish.

Monroe Fulton—whose wife was a Miss Reid—is a good citizen. He has raised a family of sons and daughters noted for their love of literature, piety and religion. His sons are preachers and lawyers.

The location for Grayson Court House was first made when Grayson and Carroll were one county—named Greenville—now known as Old Town. After the division of the county Independence was the place selected for the new county site. The location is well selected and is a pleasant place for a home. The town contains stores and print-shops. The population of the town is composed of intelligent, praiseworthy people—Doctors, lawyers, mechanics. teachers and so forth. The abundant yield of cereals, fine filavored fruits and great variety of vegetables make this county among the foremost in that line. Here you will find an inexhaustible supply of clear, cold water, salubrious air and a healthy climate. Here are beautiful country resi-

THE SANDS OF TIME. 59

dences, fine dwelling houses, mansions and palaces surrounded by lovely shade trees and flowers of richest hue, make the farmer's interest paramount to all other branches of business. It is said in holy writ that the land of Canaan flowed with milk and honey. Grayson county produces plentifully of both these articles. Christian culture in the family circle is delightfully displayed. The sweet-spirited, refined female courtesy, the affable genial, kindness of proprietors, sons and others of the residences make the christian home an earthly paradise, where the fruits of industry and economy have furnished the most luxurious festive tables, prepared by the greatest skill that female genius could present. These kind entertainments are found in many families in the county of Grayson.

Following is a biographical sketch of some prominent families and of the public services rendered by people who held official positions: Joshua Cox married Ruth Orsborn and settled on Bridle Creek, a rich and fertile valley, where nature has lavished her rich gifts and industry and art developed them. Joshua Cox was a good citizen and did much toward advancing the best interests of his neighborhood. They raised four sons and three daughters, namely: John, David, Hardin and Isom, Hannah, Jennie and Margaret. Hardin married Nacy Reeves, a zealous christian and active worker in the Methodist church. Hardin served his county as Justice of the Peace for many years and was assessor when Grayson and Carroll were one county. He was a systematic farmer. They raised a worthy family, such as is a blessing to any community. Their eldest son fell in the Confederate army, a brave soldier—honored and respected—who laid his life on his country's altar

Esquire Elbert S. Cox and family live near the old homestead. He married Miss Jane Hampton, an excellent woman. They have a son now practicing law. Joshua McGowan Cox and family live at the old family residence. They are a nice family and have a pleasant home. Enoch Cox, another brother married Susan Thomas, an amiable good woman. Their daughter, Mollie married Zechariah Orsborn, Jr., a young man of superior talents, piety and industry, who died in the prime of life leaving a widow with the care of raising a family. This lady's bright intelligence qualifies her to raise under christian culture a family of children whose superior talents promise a bright future.

John Cox, son of Joshua Cox, married Miss Nellie Ward. They raised a large family. Their son, Andrew J. Cox fell in the Confederate army an honored soldier. This noble boy's death was deeply lamented by many friends. Jesse Cox is still living. He has a good family and is himself a good citizen and neighbor. Another brother, Benjamin Cox has an excellent wife. They enjoy life in quietude and peace, wisely preparing for the enjoyment of this life and church privileges, laying up treasures in heaven. Aras B. Cox, the youngest son of this family, lives on the old homestead of his parents. He has been twice married; first to a Miss Parsons, second to Miss Lucy Boyer. He is a good citizen and has provided well for the temporal comforts of life and is laying up treasures in the christian's home in heaven. They have a nice family. Their son, Alexander and daughter, Ida, who now remain with their parents, are intelligent and pleasant young people. Their younger children are cheerful and mannerly, thus giving evidence of good family government.

There are many whose record we cannot

trace, whose lives and noble deeds are worthy of commemoration but it would crowd this work too much to put them on record, so, we will only present a few names of those who have been distinguished in temporal pursuits and official positions in public life.

Captain Joseph Phipps—who married Miss Nancy McMillan—was one of Grayson county's best farmers, a man of great energy and a successful manager of business. He acquired a handsome amount of property and raised a worthy family. He and his excellent wife went down to their graves honored, loved and respected. Joseph Bryant—whose first wife was Miss Sallie Hale—lived near Bridle Creek post office and owned a good farm cultivated under the most improved methods. He and his excellent wife were zealous members of the M. E. Church South. They raised a family of children that honored their parents and community where they lived.

Samuel Cox married Miss Elizabeth Thomas. They lived near Bridle Creek. He and his amiable christian wife were advocates of education and contributed to its success as far as they could with limited opportunities- They owned a pleasant home and raised an intelligent and worthy family of children.

Enoch Ward and family lived up in the coves on the south side of Buck mountain. He was a harmless man of genial kindness and loved for friends to visit him in his isolated home. They farmed and cultivated bees, and when friends visited them not only gave them freely of the honey but would have them go in the room where the honey was stored away and lift the cans of strained honey. But these good old people have gone to their graves. Peace to their quiet rest.

One of the greatest improvements in this part of the county is Bridle Creek Academy, boarding houses and fine churches. It is a locality of beautiful farms and orchards. fine family residences, and a population of enlightened christian people. Board—with well furnished tables and good lodging—can be obtained at reasonable rates. Professor Gardner has conducted this academy with entire satisfaction to students, parents and guardians, and the institution continues to grow in interest and usefulness.

We have given a statement of some of the prominent families that first settled in Grayson county with events of their day. There are certain facts we have carefully culled—

true and reliable—that are worthy of record on the golden pages of history that many people with little patriotic love of country and its bright early history will regard as small things, but they will give the pleasing recollection of what principle with perseverance will accomplish. The people of Grayson county were made up of friends of the colonists and were true to the principles of liberty and justice.

In reviewing the history of the past, when the people, through hardships, privations and toils, laid the foundation for higher degrees of happiness and richer states of enjoyment, we contrast the past with the present condition of Bridle Creek settlement when it was made up of a few emigrants in a wild, indian country, with their only trust in a kind Providence and a little fort for defense, with the noble spirit of martyrs and the present condition—with an institution of learning, fine buildings, academy, church, boarding-houses. well qualified professors and teachers. under strict moral and religious government, surrounded by rich farms, beautiful dwellings and refined society. What great cause for us to lift up our hearts to God in grateful remembrance for such ancestors; who sacrificed

THE SANDS OF TIME. 65

so much; who paved the way for what we now enjoy!

Advancement from lower to higher degrees has characterized the physical, mental and moral universe of God. Human instrumentalities are employed to carry out the great work of art and science for the establishment of human happiness. When we consider the fact that the seeds of moral excellence were sown in the hearts of children by parents that would blossom and bear fruit in after years we are thankful to our ancestors. We select a few out of the many worthy people who labored with each other and deserve the highest praise.

Isom Cox—who married Miss Jincey Phipps, an accomplished, intelligent lady; an ornament to her home and a blessing to her family—was one of Grayson county's best citzens and largest farmers. He owned the land where Bridle Creek academy and church are located. Isom Cox did much for church and state. He was ever ready to assist in any laudable enterprise for the good of society. He and his faithful wife were members of the Methodist church South. Their example was a priceless heritage to their children. The children have honored their parents by following both precept and example. Their only two sons, Haywood and Jasper fell in the Confederate army. Nobler young men and better soldiers never honored an army or country.

Columbus Phipps married Nannie daughter of Isom and Jincey Cox. Mr. Phipps has used more than ordinary energy in all that pertains to temporal business and religious duties. His faithful services as superintendent of the Sunday school has done much to advance the number of its members and interest—a work of so much importance in training the minds and habits of life in successful pursuit of temporal business and preparation for the rest, association and bliss of heaven. The home of Mr. Phipps and excellent family shows what industry and economy can do He has a fine farm, improved stock and stately dwellings. His hope of a mansion in the better world is well founded. what deep gratitude we should feel to the giver of every good and perfect gift and rewarder of them that diligently seek him.

Captain Melville B. Cox, a prominent citizen has contributed much to every laudable enterprise for the improvement of his country and good of society. His wife was Miss Martha Fulton, a lady of cultivated intellect and refinement. Captain Cox is a successful farmer, proprietor of a fine mercantile flour mill, dealer in live stock, and has assisted materially in establishing Bridle Creek Academy. His son, Joseph Cox has been an efficient teacher in the academy and has for some time been a law student in Washington City, where he took the highest degree on examination in a class with Yale and Harvard students (so I am informed). Captain Cox and wife are devoted members of the Methodist church South. Their example in the family circle and community will live when they are gone from time, having assisted other good people with whom they associated in this life to obey the counsel of the great apostle to the Gentile, "Let us go on to perfection."

In summing up the biographical sketches of the lives of people and lineal decendants of ancestors there are many whose lives and labors we would like to record but the limits of this work will not admit. We will, however, give briefly a limited list of some of the citizens—people that have been an honor to the country and blessing to the community. Enoch Orsborn, Jr., was an example of moral excellence. He married Jincey Burton, a lady of deep piety, a faithful wife and affectionate mother. Soloman Orsborn who, in an eminent degree, was what has been styled the noblest work of God, was an honest man. His amiable christian wife who, before her marriage was Hannah Cox, enjoyed with their family a happy home on the Old Fort farm. Esquire David Cox married Miss Jane Doughton, a patien, quiet good christian and faithful good wife and affectionate mother. Hon. Fielding J. Hale, state senator from Madison, Nebraska, is their grandson.

John H. Perkins and family resided in this county, a good neighbor and worthy citizen. Robert Pugh—who married a Miss Thomas—was a good and upright citizen and raised a family of children that did honor to parents and county. Ezekiel Young, of Wilson Creek, married Miss Eveline McMillan and raised an excellent family. Mr. Young and amiable wife and most of their children, many in number, were zealous, faithful members of the Methodist church South and did much to establish piety and religion in their neighborhood. These good parents have gone to reap their rich reward on the other side of the river in the christian's home in heaven.

Esquire William Grubb and kind wife and worthy family lived on the road near the mountain leading from the mouth of Wilson to Marion, Va. He was an upright man. He and his amiable wife raised a good family. Many a wearied traveler rested in their hospitable home of entertainment. Gordon Perkins married a Miss Stamper and lived on Wilson Creek. They were good people and raised a worthy family.

Fielding Young married Miss Rena Phipps, daughter of Captain Joseph Phipps. He and his devoted wife were members of the Methodist church South. They took an active part in preparing to entertain the people who attended the meeting at the old Wilson camp-meeting ground. While listening to the proclamation of the gospel delivered in eloquence and power, the weeping of mourners, shouts of converts and praises to God from christians thrilled the soul with ecstacy and joy.

Colonel Stephen Hale, of Elk Creek, married Miss Charlotte Dickerson, a christian lady who adorned the family circle. She offered up public prayer and delivered earnest exhortations. Col. Hale and wife and most of their family were devoted members of the Methodist church South. If every family lived as Mr. Hales' lived this would be a happy world. There would be no need of jails or penitentiaries, and we would not be taxed so high. Col. Hale married the second time Mrs. Mitchell who was a noble christian woman, and one who gave peace and happiness, in the love of God, to the home of these good people, where their sun of life sat beneath a cloudless sky to rise in the resurrection morn.

Col. Eli Cornette, of Elk Creek, was a leading citizen. He and his excellent wife raised a worthy family. The Colonel's nephew, George W. Cornette married Miss Sarah Gentry, daughter of Col. Allen and Rebecca Gentry, of N. C., just such a lady as will make a contented husband and happy home. Judge Cornette has filled several offices with honor to himself and satisfaction to his people.

Samuel Cox, Jr., resides on the old homestead where his parents, Samuel Cox, Sr., and faithful good wife lived. Samuel Cox, Jr., married Miss Phebe Orsborn.—(Phebe, a name venerated from the servant of Cenchrea who carried St Paul's epistle to the Romans from Corinth to Rome.) Mr. Cox and brothers, Alexander and Callaway married sisters. They and their families live in the same neighborhood near the mouth of Little River, true types of their patriotic ancestors.

THE SANDS OF TIME. 71

George Reeves, Sr., and family came from Drury's Bluff, below Richmond, settled on New River, some five or six miles southeast of Independence where they remained to the close of life. Their sons were Jesse, William, George and John, their daughters Anna, Charity, Mary and Susan. Jesse married a Miss Terrell and moved to the mouth of Peak Creek on New River, Ashe county, N. C., on a farm made by old Mr. Dick, one of the first settlers of the county. William Reeves also married a Miss Terrell and moved to Alleghany county, N. C., (as it now is). George Reeves married Miss Jane Orsborn, a woman possessed of a high order of talent, genial disposition, industrious habits, kindhearted and pious. Mr. Reeves moved to where Esquire Charles H. Doughton and son, Rev. J. B. Doughton now live. He was an energetic business man, and while serving his county as an officer excecuted some horses and was carrying them away when the owner followed and shot and mortally wounded him. He left a widow and seven children, Jesse, Enoch, George, Mary, Nancy, Rebecca and Cynthia. John Reeves married Miss Phebe Orsborn, of whom it may be truly said, was a true type of womanhood in all that was good and lovely. Mr. Reeves and family occupied the old homestead. Mr. Reeves not only left a good home for his family but a richer legacy, that of industry, prudence, economy and honesty. His pious christian wife was ever a treasury of love. John Reeves and excellent wife raised a family to be proud of. Rev. Orsborn Reeves married Rebecca Orsborn, of whom it may well be said, was truly a helpmeet. The cheerful face, pleasant expression, kind words, and neat dwelling made their home a home of joy and comfort. Mr. Reeves was a preacher and Elder in the Protestant Methodist church. Their son, John Reeves, a boy soldier fell in the Confederate army. The testament in his left vest pocket was cut through with the bullet that took his life. His immortal spirit took its flight to realms of bliss, where no battle-scarred, patriotic, country-loving soldier boy's body will ever suffer, but will stand with the snow-white army of the redeemed to adore, to all eternity, the Captain-General of the world's salvation. Mr. Reeves and family lived in Georgia, not far from Cave Springs but some years later moved West. Col. George W. Reeves and family lived many years in Ashe county, N. C., to which we will refer later. Jesse A. Reeves married his cousin, Miss Charity Reeves, and lived in Ashe county, N. C. John Reeves, Jr., the youngest son married Miss Mary Reeves, an amiable young woman, and resided with the old people. He had the honor and pleasing task of taking care of his parents in the evening of life Mr. Reeves died when comparatively a young man. His body, with his father, John Reeves, Sr., and sainted wife and mother rests in the family graveyard to await the shrill whisile of Gabriel's trumpet to call them in the resurrection morn.

Preston Reeves, son of John and widow, Polly Reeves married Elizabeth. daughter of Isom and Jincey Cox. Mr. Reeves and worthy wife, by prudence and economy have provided well for home and comforts of life. They are an honor to family s and country. Captain Taliaferro Witcher married Miss Jane Reeves and moved to N. C. His life and public services will be treated in their proper places. Miss Lucy Reeves married Esquire James Gambill. Miss Mahala Reeves married Rev. Samuel Plummer. Miss Polly Reeves married Marshall Callaway.

Troy Cox, his brothers and family were worthy citizens and good people. Hardin Cox and devoted christian wife, a talented, accomplished lady lived on Potato Creek. His fine dwelling house, buildings and well regulated farm on Potato Creek stand as a monument of industry and economy. He was a useful laborer in church and state. He died in manhood's prime, and his happy spirit has gone to dwell in the christian's home above where it awaits the arrival of loved ones. The widow, Emeline Cox, son Charles and amiable wife and family live happily in their home of beauty and comfort—the fruit of their labor. John D. Cox, estimable wife and family live on Potato Creek. Mr. Cox is a practical farmer and good citizen. The Graham brothers are merchants—one on Potato Creek whose wife is a daughter of Hardin and Emeline Cox, the other, Wallace Graham has a store near Saddle post office. His wife was the daughter of Stephen and Masie Bryant. She adorns her home by her social, quiet life. He and his wife are devoted members of the Methodist church. These merchants and families materially help in making the community successful, prosperous and happy.

There have been a number of ministers of the gospel who lived and labored for the moral and spiritual welfare of the people of Grayson county, whose names are entitled to record, namely: Elder Drury Senter, Rev. William Carico, Elder Plummer and Rev. Samuel Plummer, Elder Calvin Jones, Rev. Joshua Cole and Rev. James Bedwell. These servants of the church and their people have gone to receive the welcome applaudit, "Well done good and faithful servant, enter the joys of the Lord."

The history of Grayson county is such that the present and future population of the county may look back on its record with pleasure and cherish bright hopes for its future prosperity and happiness.

NOTE.—Erratum in second line on page 66 of this chapter.—The name Jasper should be Joseph.

CHAPTER VI.

NORTH-WESTERN NORTH CAROLINA.

ALLEGHANY COUNTY.

It is refreshing and a source of pleasure to every American who loves home and country that such men as Sir Walter Raleigh and Jonn Smith lived, and that this country was settled by men knowing their rights dared maintain them.

Greece believed their founders were divine; Rome delighted in the fanciful idea that her Romulus decended from the Gods. No Norman tyrant landed on our shores, nor did any fabled fugitive from the flames of Troy settle this country.

North Carolina claims to be the place where this great Anglo-Saxon Empire was born and rocked in the cradle of liberty.

THE SANDS OF TIME. 77

Here too, on the 13th of July, 1584, the first English vessels landed; and here was found a people gentle, loving, faithful and kind. Virginia dates her first settlement back to 1608; Massachusettes the landing of the Pilgrims on Plymouth Rock 1620. North Carolina was the first state on whose borders the blood of colonists was first shed by English troops, occurring at Alamance 1771, and the first state to throw off the English yoke, at Chrrlotte, 1775. North Carolina has been true to principle. It was a North Carolinian—Ensign Worth Bagley—whose blood was first spilt in defense of Cuba against Spanish injustice and cruelty. North Carolina is proud of her record. She takes her stand in the sisterhood of states and rejoices to be united with them in a government containing the principles set forth in the Declaration of Independence and constitution of the United States, one of the best countries the sun ever shone on.

North-western North Carolina is embraced in that portion of the state bounded on the south by Pilot and Brushy mountains, on the south west by Blue Ridge and Black mountain, west by Tennessee line, north by the Virginia line, containing an area beautiful and lovely—its towering mountains, green valleys, crystal streams of water, beautiful forests, rich delicious fruits, charming flowers of exquisite beauty and richest hues and exhilarating odors, and its refreshing atmosphere. It is not strange that emigrants sought a home in this highly favored land where nature placed so many attractive powers.

The products are wheat, corn, rye, oats buckwheat, potatoes, flax, sorgum cane, tobacco, cotton and fruits, also garden vegetables of luxurious growth and fine flavor. Wild birds are numerous and their charming notes help make nature more grand. What cause for gratitude to an infinite, all-wise loving Father in Heaven for such inestimable blessings.

We present by counties a description of the treasuries placed by nature that lay slumbering through the ages of the past waitnig for the magic art of civilization to develop its vast resources and change the wild forests to fuitful fields.

Alleghany county was formed from the eastern part of Ashe county. It is bounded on the south by Blue Ridge and Wilkes county line, west by Ashe county, north by the Virginia line and east by Surry county line. The county is divided into two valleys, Peach Bottom mountain passing through the county from east to west, valley of Little River on the south, New River and tributary streams, Prather's Creek and Elk Creek on the north. The surface is uneven, ridges and valleys along the streams of water, beautiful springs gushing and gurgling from hills and dales, forests of trees such as oak, pine, poplar, maple, ashe, hickory, chestnut, abundance of granite and fine species of soap-stone rich mines of iron, and copper. The productions are wheat, rye, corn, oats, buckwheat, sorgum-cane, flax, potatoes and garden vegetables of great variety that mature in luxury and perfection, fruits, such as apples, peaches, pears, quinces, plums, cherries. blackberries, strawberries, currants, whortleberries and grapes.

Alleghany county's history is such that any patriotic, country-loving people may justly be proud of and look to for a bright future. The early settlers of this county were made up partly from eastern counties of North Carolina, some from Virginia and other states, and emigrants from Europe. They had learned by experience what oppressive laws, exorbitant taxation and injustice was. They came here imbued with the principles of liberty and justice and with determination to free themselves and posterity from under the iron wheel of tyranny, and were characterized by industry, economy and moral excellence They labored not in vain. The present lineal descendants can look back with pleasing reflections that in the providence of an all-wise God of love and justice an enlightened christian people made their homes here and erected the standard of liberty and also the standard of the Cross of Him whose Word says, "Be diligent in business, fervent in spirit, serving the Lord." Shall the names of those who periled their lives, and toiled, enduring the privations of a wild, indian country, for the happy enjoyment of the inhabitants who live afterward, be forgotten and not preserved in history? Never! Let the spirit of patriotic love of home and country live and live on, and streams of salvation flow as does the limpid stream over its sandy bed.

Sparta is the county capital, a most beautiful location, admirably arranged in streets, business houses, residences, hotels, churches, academy, law and medical offices, furniture manufactory and one of the best printing-presses, with job department and general publishing office, in Western North Carolina. The

Alleghany Star is published here. It is an excellent paper giving local news of interest and much general news. It is a popular paper with a reading circulation of 20,000. Attached to the printing office is a wholesale store of stationery which is a great convenience to this part of the state.

Prof. S. W. Brown resides here and is an able minister of the gospel of the Methodist church South and principal of the academy. His faithful labors in the ministry and success as a teacher has won for him the approval and respect of the country.

This work is intended more as a biographical than descriptive history, endeavoring with much care to make from the best sources of information true statements of both people and country. The following is a list of some of the names of the early settlers of Alleghany county:

Williamses, Woodruffs, Bryans, McMillans, Edwardses, Burtons, Doughtons, Crouses and Fenders. Francis Bryan came to Alleghany county from Elk Creek, Va., but originally from the eastern part of the state. He married Miss Phebe Woodruff and settled in the south-eastern part of the county on the road leading from Grayson Old Town to Traphill, Wilkes county, where he and family lived to a good old age. Mr. Bryan was a good citizen and kind neighbor who took much interest in the prosperity, happiness and general welfare of the people. He represented his county in the legislature in 1818. His family were distinguished for their energy and perseverance in business relations of life. After a long life of toil and doing good Mr. Bryan and noble wife, loved and respected, were placed in their honored graves where they now rest in peaceful sleep.

John McMillan, a native of Scotland, and a man of letters, came to Alleghany county and settled on Elk Creek. He brought his excellent wife with him from Scotland. He was an extensive farmer and good citizen and was first clerk of Ashe county. His family had the industry and watchful care in business affairs peculiar to their nationality. Their sons were Andrew, James, John and Alexander, their daughters Nancy, Mazy and Mary. Andrew married a Miss Fields and moved to Ashe county. John married Miss Cessa Gambill and raised a very worthy family of children.

Jonh Burton married a Miss Stamper and raised a worthy family. William Harbor was the first manufacturer of iron in the county. One of his daughters, an estimable lady, married Hon. Richard Gentry, of Ashe county. His sons went West. Sabe Choat married a Miss Woodfork and moved from Wilkes county to Bush Creek, Alleghany county. They raised one of the most energetic business families in all this country. Their sons, Isom and Thomas Choat went to Georgia, were planters and speculators and became wealthy. Richard Choat married Miss Sallie Edwards, a lady possessed of all the enobling virtues that adorn female character, as daughter, sister, wife and mother, such as make happy homes worth living for. One of their daughters married David Edwards and lived in Wilkes county and another daughter married David Isom, of Grayson county, Va.

William Edwards and David Edwards were settlers of Alleghany county at an early date and did a good part in establishing good society, bringing about success and prosperity, and in advancing the best interests of their country. David Edwards, son of William Edwards, was a worthy citizen of Wilkes county.

Currin Elliott, of Hillsville, Carroll county, Va., married the daughter of David Edwards.

Stephen Wilkerson, of Hillsville, also married his daughter. Both are ornaments to their home and an honor to their families. One of William Edwards, Sr's. daughters, married Allen Fender, of whom it may correctly be said, not lived for themselves only, but for the good of others. They raised a family that did honor to their parents and country. Their son, John Fender, whose excellent wife was Captain Daniel Whitehead's daughter, was an honored soldier in the Confederate army and filled a commissary office with patience, skill and honest care that honored his head and heart. Mr. Fender is now a citizen of Peak Creek, Ashe county. They have a worthy family of children. David Edwards, Sr., the the pioneer settler of Alleghany county, represented the county of Ashe in the legislature of North Carolina when Alleghany, Ashe and Watauga were one county in 1812. Mr. Edwards lived on Little River for some years. His first wife was a Miss Anders. They raised a large family noted for industry, economy, perseverance and prudence in business relations. Their son, Esquire Berry Edwards was a leading citizen of Alleghany county and one of its best financial officers. Esquire Edwards' son, David was an honored soldier in

the Confederate army. In his early life he
spent six years in the California gold region.
He married Miss Mattie Reeves. By industry and economy they have acquired a handsome amount of property. They have an intelligent, interesting family of children. Esquire Senter Edwards, a brother of David
Edwards, married Miss Jane Choat, a charming good lady, wife and mother, a good neighbor and christian friend. Their son, Reed,
is the present Sheriff of Alleghany county.
Esquire Senter Edwards is one of the county's
best citizens and peace officers.

David Edwards, Sr., married the second
time Mrs. Jane Reeves, widow of George
Reeves. They had two children after second
marriage, and lived on Elk Creek on the old
homestead where the widow Reeves resided
before her second marriage. Their son Solomon O. lives in the same neighborhood, a worthy and respected citizen. He married Miss
Amazie McMillan, a kind-hearted amiable good
woman, a devoted wife and affectionate mother, kind neighbor and faithful friend. Their
daughter, Phebe Edwards, was the wife of the
author of these sketches whose life will be
given in a separate statement of her family
history. David Edwards, Sr., an example of in-

dustry, moral worth, and sainted wife, having faithfully done their part as good people in the various relations of life, now rest in their honored graves, in the family graveyard on the same farm.

Joseph Doughton was one of the original settlers of the county and came here from Franklin county, Virginia. He married a Miss Reeves and lived in the north-eastern part of the county. He was a farmer and mechanic. He represented his county in the Legislature of 1817. Was respected as an upright citizen, whose honesty and integrity in the discharge of his duty, in the faithful performance in whatever was intrusted to his care. Esquire Charles H. Doughton is their son and an honored citizen, yet living, almost one hundred years old. He has served his county as Justice of the Peace; also county surveyor and is a practical farmer and livestock raiser. He married widow Margaret Reeves and raised a worthy, excellent family. Their sons, Fleming and Jesse, are in Oergon. Fleming Doughton married Colonel Petty's daughter, of Wilkes county, a most excellent lady. Esquire Doughton and his devoted (now deceased) wife are and were members of the Methodist church from early life. Mrs.

Doughton has been dead for many years. They were liberal supporters of the church in its various enterprises. Their son, Rev. Josesh B. Doughton, is a local Methodist preacher, whose faithful labor in assisting his preaching brethren in the great work of building up the Redeemer's kingdom—a work of such responsibility, rising paramount above all other employments—beating back the power of darkness and works of evil, and establishing peace and righteousness and happy homes in the family circle, where the love of God thrills the soul and communities rejoice together at the house of God in hopes of spending together in heaven an eternity of bliss and happiness.

A daughter of Joseph Doughton, Jr. married George Reeves and moved to Winterset, Iowa. Her daughter, Sophrona, married Alfred D. Jones who was secretary for the first Territorial Governor of Nebraska, and settled in Omaha. Mr. Jones is one of the principal founders of the beautiful city of Omaha which has grown up and increased in population with a rapidity that tells its location is surrounded by one of the richest producing countries on earth, with railroad and steamboat facilities. The Burlington and

Missouri River railroad trains supplied with reclining chairs, accommodating employers, conveying passengers over its many branches through the Western states, has been the greatest agency in building up that section.

Solomon Parsons, John Jones, Daniel Jones, Tobias Long, John Long and Jobe Stamper may properly be classed with the elder men and early settlers of Alleghany county. Alexander B. McMillan, son of John McMillan, Sr., married Miss Mary Reeves, an excellent, intelligent good woman, and lived on the old homestead on Elk Creek. He was a successful, practical farmer and a good financial officer of his county who represented the county, when Ashe, Alleghany and Watauga were one county, in both branches of the legislature. Esquire McMillan was a true patriot. As a citizen he discharged his duty faithfully and with honor to himself and satisfaction to his people, both in public office and private life. Esquire McMillan and noble wife were members of the Baptist church. Their bodies now rest in their honored graves in the family graveyard. Franklin B. McMillan, their only son, was educated at Emory and Henry college in Virginia and graduated in law at the University of North Carolina.

He was a young man of bright intellect, and professed religion in early life. His moral excellence, social disposition and genial kindness gained for him the popular good will and highest respect of the people. He married Miss Susan Dodge, a young lady of a high order of talents, education and refinement. It was a happy union. They were blessed with one child that died in infancy. Both husband and wife died in early life. They were sadly missed by their friends and acquaintances.

Colonel Allen Gentry was a citizen of Alleghany county, a public-spirited gentleman who took an active part in every laudable enterprise for the good of his country. He was a practical farmer, merchant, Justice of the Peace and representative in the legislature of North Carolina. It was through his influence that Alleghany couuty was created. He was a true patriot that loved his country and labored for its good. He was a kind husband, affectionate father, zealous, faithful christian member of the Methodist church South. His many friends lamented his death which occurred in the prime of life, at a time when his valuable services were most needed by his family and country. Col. Gentry married

Miss Rebecca Reeves, who possessed in an eminent degree the social virtues of a pure heart that elevates woman to her proper sphere, as daughter, sister, wife, mother, kind neighbor and christian friend, such as make happy homes and good society. She was a sainted wife whose duty shined with brilliancy on life's pathway. She and her husband were devoted members of the Methodist church South. Their bodies rest side by side in their honored graves at Shiloh-church graveyard. Dr. L. C. Gentry, of Ashe county, and Captain George W. Centry, of Stephenville, Tex , are their sons. He was an honored cavalry officer in the Confederate army. also a farmer and wholesale merchant. His wife was a Miss Whitiman, a most excellent lady. Their daughter, Miss Sarah. married Judge George W. Cornette, of Grayson county, Virginia. Cynthia married Captain James H. Parks, a merchant and honored citizen who died some years ago. His amiable wife is still living. They were worthy members of the Methodist church South. Mattie married Rev. J. B. Doughton. She possessed the enobling virtues that make a preacher a good wife. Ellen married William Hardin, a worthy gentleman. She was a true type of industry, kindness and affection. They both have passed away from the scenes of earth, leaving with their friends evidence that they have gone to join loved ones on the other side of the river.

Hon. Abram Bryan, son of Hon. Francis and Phebe Bryan, married Mrs. Woodruff, formerly Miss Carter. They lived on the old homestead of his parents. Mr. Bryan was truly a good man. His moral, upright life and patriotic love of country and devotion to its best interests, his honest, strict integrity and social disposition gave him the popular good will of the people. He was representative in the senate of the state legislature, served as Justice of the Peace for many years was cartful to preserve order in his community. If all persons would live as Abram Bryan lived there would be no guilty to prosecute nor need of defense for the innocent.

Morgan Bryan was a practical farmer and earnest local Methodist preacher. He married Miss Susan Hale, an amiable, good christian lady. William Bryan, who moved to Surry county, was a local Methodist preacher and a man of much moral worth who raised a wortby family. Shadrack Bryan, grandson of Francis Brown, Sr., was a good citizen, of marked industry and a quiet good man. He was a local Methodist minister. He married his cousin, a charming, good lady, and raised a nice family.

John Fender, Sr., was a good citizen. His wife was a Miss Toliver, a worthy, good woman. They raised a most excellent family. Zechariah and Thomas Moxley were good citizens and raised worthy families. Moses Dixon was a worthy, respectable citizen. He married Miss Sarah Orsborne and raised a large family whose lineal descendants are scattered far West. They were a persevering and industrious family.

Robert Thompson, an iron manufacturer on Little River, was a very industrious useful man. He supplied the country for a distance around with that article which was so important to producers. Mr. Thompson married a Miss Harbard and raised a praiseworthy family. Major Samuel Thompson, their son, married a Miss Dickey, an excellent lady. They made their home in the same neighborborhood.

William Woodruff, a noble citizen, married a Miss Thompson, a lady worthy her husband. Mr. Woodruff has been dead many years. His widow married the second time Judge

John Gambill who, as a citizen and county
officer, was an honor to his county and people.
He is also dead, leaving his amiable wife a
widow the second time. She too is dead.

George Reeves, grandson of George
Reeves. Sr., was one of Alleghany county's
best citizens. He married Miss Nancy Fields,
who was a faithful wife, kind mother and
charitable neighbor George Reeves was a
conscientious christian, had great respect for
truth and a good, trustworthy neighbor
They raised a family, some of whom and their
descendants, have been distinguished for
talents and worthy lives. Their grandson,
G. A. Oglesby, is a talented minister of the
gospel, member of the North Carolina annual
conference of the M. E. church, South. Horton Reeves was an honored soldier in the Confederate army, clerk of Alleghany county and
now a citizen of Texas. His wife was Miss
Nancy Alexander, an amiable lady.

F. M. Mitchell. grandson of James
Gwyn, of Wilkes county, married Miss
Caroline Alexander, a faithful wife, affectionate mother and kind neighbor. Mr. Mitchell
was an honorable soldier in the Confederate
army, where he lost a leg. He is a good citizen and has been county register for many

years. Captain Daniel Whitehead was one of Alleghany county's best citizens. He married a Miss Crouse and lived where Whitehead Academy and village is located.

Captain John R. Long, of Cranberry, married a Miss Asher. He was an enterprising citizen of industry and economy and raised an intelligent family. Hon. Caswell Taylor married their daughter and raised a nice family, characterized by energy, industry and perseverance in business departments. Mr. Taylor has represented his county in the state legislature.

Elder Tobias Long was an earnest, zealous, Baptist preacher, a good man by example and precept. John Long. his brother, was a member of the denomination known as the Christian church. He was ordained by his church and preached occasionally. Dr. Solomon Long, a native and resident of Meadow Fork, Cranberry, and a graduate of Jeffersonian College, Philadelphia. These two brothers, Tobias and John, also lived on Meadow Fork.

Captain Horton Doughton is an excellent citizen of Alleghany county. He married Miss Rebecca Jones and raised a family that honors parents and country. Captain Doughton was an honored soldier in the Confederate army. He is a public-spirited gentleman who has looked with vigilant care and aided in carrying out successfully the best interests of his country. He is a good financial agent and has served as Justice of the Peace for years.

Dr. B. C. Waddell is a graduate of Baltimore Medical College. He resides at Scottville, in the western part of the county. Dr. B. C. Waddell is a young man of a high order of talents. The interest he takes in devoting his time and services in practicing his profession, attending calls day or night, mild or inclement weather, kind and pleasant attention to patients, success in practice, has given him an enviable reputation. He married Miss Melissa Baldwin, a lady of intelligence and refinement. They are both pious christians. Dr. George D. Mendinhall practiced his profession in Alleghany county a few years. He is a well qualified and successful physician. Dr. C. G. Foulkes has done considerable practice but is worn out with age and no longer able to wait on his friends as their physician as he once did.

William Black came from Scotland. He married a Miss Allison and settled near where Mt. Zion church now stands, in the western part of the county. He was an earnest, devoted christian. They raised a family of much moral excellence and christian virtues. Their sons were John, Alexander and David, their daughters, Jennie, Martha, Elizabeth and Mary. John Black married Miss Mary Reedy. Andrew and Lee are their sons; noble men, who have worthy families. Major David Black married a Miss King. They had one child. Mrs. Black died in early life, and the Major married the second time Miss Rena Cox, daughter of Troy Cox, of Virginia. They had one son, Troy, an aspiring, worthy young man. Major Black died in the prime of life. His widow married again and is still living, a noble christian lady. Alexander Black married Miss Matilda Hampton. They have one son, Oscar, a young man of bright intellect and promise of a useful life. Their family is an example of prosperity, peaceful enjoyment and christian happiness. Martha Black married Harrison Stamper who lives near Laurel Springs. These good people have given their aid freely to the Methodist church, especially in erecting a house of worship, for which they deserve the thanks of the community. Elizabeth Black married David Pugh, a worthy citizen. She died in early life.

Mary Black married Daniel Taylor, Jr. They live near Sparta and are a worthy family. Jennie Black married James Reedy who died many years ago. The widow sitill lives in the neighborhood of Mt Zion. Their sons, Lee and Andrew, are honored citizens. The ancestor, William Black, has gone from his labors on earth to reap his reward in heaven, but the seed he sowed are bearing rich fruits in a neighborhood of the best society in the county. David Gilham, native of Floyd county, Va., married Miss Mary Howell and lived near Gap Civil. He was a manufacturer of leather, and was an honest, upright citizen. They raised a worthy family. Their son, George, was an honored soldier in the Confederate army. Another son, Wesley, is a prominent member of the Methodist church and a worthy citizen. Eld. George Douglass was an early settler of this county. He was a talented, eloquent minister of Baptist church and served his people faithfully for many years. His influence will live and live on. Elder Solomon Stamper, of Cranberry, a Baptist minister, inclined to be eccentric and humorous, sound in doctrine, fervent in spirit, honored and respected, served his generation faithfully, laid down the silver trumpet for a harp in heaven.

EX-LIEUT-GOV. RUFUS A. DOUGHTON.

THE SANDS OF TIME. 99

Hon. Rufus A. Doughton is a native of Alleghany county. He was born near Laurel Springs Jan. 10th, 1856, and was educated at the High School at Independence, Va , and at the University of North Carolina. at which place he graduated in law during June, 1880. Since that time he has practiced his profession with much success. He was married January the 2nd, 1883, to Miss Sue Parks, and has one son, Kemp, and one danghter, Miss Annie. He was county superintendent of schools in 1883, and in 1887 was elected to the House of Representatives He was re-elected in 1889 and served as chairman of the committee on education. He was again elected in 1891 and chosen speaker of the House. At the Democratic State convention, in 1892, he was nominated for the second highest state office, and in November elected by a majority of more than forty thousand over his Republican opponant. In 1892 and 1897 he received the nomination of the Democratic party in the legislature for the United States Senate. He is, and has been for a number of years, truster of the University of North Carolina. In early life he bowed at the shrine of knowledge and employed all the powers of his active mind in acquiring knowledge that would prepare him to serve his country in all that would promote its happiness, prosperity and future welfare. He is a Democrat from principle, but not intolerant with those who differ from him in political sentiment. He is yet a young man and has much promise of usefulness to the state.

Hon. Richard Williams was one of the first settlers of Alleghany county. He was representative in the legislature from 1801 to 1811. He possessed the wisdom and patriotic love of country to govern successfully the newly settled colony. His valuable life and faithful services are worthy a place on the records of history.

James Boyer was one of Alleghany's best citizens. His wife was a Miss Sutherland, of Grayson county, Va., an excellent christian lady. Alexander Hampton lived in the same neighborhood. His first wife was a Miss Fulton, his second wife a Miss Sutherland. Their son, Rev. Lee Hampton, is an earnest faithful laborer in the church. His sister, Lucinda, an invalid, is a young lady of fine intellectual powers of mind, a pious christian, giving evidence of the comforts of religion in the hour of affliction, that will work a far more exeeding weight of glory.

David Maxwell was an industrious, good citizen. He married Mrs. Mary Fields who was a Miss McMillan before her first marriage. They had one son, a kind-hearted, worthy good man, respected by the community, was cruelly murdered by Bushwhackers in time of war. His wife was Jane Edwards, a good woman and faithful wife. They had two children, daughter, Laura, and son, Wiley.

Floyd Cox is a citizen of Alleghany. He married Miss Cinthia Reeves. whose quiet, christian life and faithful devotion to the best interests of her frmily's welfare and happiness does credit to her head and heart. Cloyd Cox has been a practical farmer and good citizen and obliging neighbor. Their son, Wiley, married Miss Laura Maxwell, an intelligent lady, a faithful wife, affectionate mother and kind neighbor. Mr. Cox has served his county as superior court Clerk for a number of years. Julia Cox, their daughter, married LaFayette Williams, an active business man, hotel keeper at Sparta and also a farmer. They have one son, Edgar. an aspiring young man of promise. This family is a model of industry, prudence and economy, quietude and happiness.

William Carson emigrated from Ireland

and settled in Charlotte, N. C., engaged in cotton speculation at an early age and became wealthy. He lived to a good, old age. His brothers, John and Andrew, came to North Carolina and settled in Ashe, now Alleghany county. Their families were intelligent, enterprising business people. John Carson's son, Thomas, married a Miss Thompson, whose son, Robert, was Clerk of Alleghany county for several years. Another son, Andrew Carson married Miss Emma Boyers and lived in Sparta. Alexander S. Carson, editor of the Alleghany Star, is their son. His sister, Miss Ellen, is a talented young lady, whose capacity for business has but few equals and no superiors. Another sister, Miss Emma, is also a talented, accomplished and charming young lady. Andrew Carson. Sr., son of John M. Carson, was Sheriff of Ashe county many years and merchandised at Jefferson.

Eugene Transom married Miss Laura Cheek, an accomplished lady and lives on Elk Creek. He is one of the best farmers in the county, and is also a dealer in live stock. Prof. John M. Cheek, A. M., is a native and citizen of Alleghany county. He married Miss Mollie, daughter of Judge W. Cornett, of

Virginia, a lady of culture and refinement. Prof. Cheek is one of the country's most useful men.

Profs. E L. Wagoner, J. T. Fender, W. R. Gentry, as Principals of institutions of learning, have done much for the cause of education. The people of Alleghany county deserve much credit for the interest they are taking in the cause of education. Sparta Institute. under the leadership of Professor S. W. Brown as Principal, is an honor to the county.

Dr. John Smith was a worthy citizen of Alleghany county, married Miss Bettie Hawthorne, an excellent, good woman, practiced his profession successfully for many years, was an officer in the Confederate army, and lost an arm. He represented his county in the legislature.

William Hardin was a lawyer, married Miss Ellen Gentry, a most excellent lady. They lived in Sparta and raised an intelligent, energetic family.

Alleghany county has much reason to rejoice in the history of its past and cherish bright hopes for the future.

CHAPTER VII.

NORTH-WESTERN NORTH CAROLINA.

Ashe County.

Ashe county was formed in 1799 from that portion of Wilkes lying west of the extreme height of the Appalachian mountains or Blue Ridge. It is the extreme North-west corner of the state, and bounded on the north by the Virginia line, east by the line separating it from Alleghany, south by the Blue Ridge, which separates it from Wilkes and Watauga, west by Tennessee line, separating it from Johnson county. It was called in honor of Samuel Ashe who was once Governor of the state.

Its surface is uneven, hills and ridges and intervening valleys along the creeks and rivers. The supply of water is abundant.

The north and south forks of New River pass through the county with their tributary streams. There is scarcely a plat of land to be found large enough for an ordinary farm that is not supplied with springs of clear, cold water and streams running through them. The productions are wheat, rye, corn, oats, buckwheat, sorgum-cane, tobacco, potatoes, flax, and a great variety of garden vegetables. The fruit-productions are apples, peaches, pears, quinces and plums, with many varities of small fruits, such as cherries, currants, blackberries, strawberries, cranberries, whortleberries and gooseberries. Beautiful groves of timber, oak, hickory, ash, poplar, maple, walnut, pine and cherry. The climate and soil is well adapted to the growth of different grasses, as timothy, clover, redtop, bluegrass and evergreen.

Jefferson, the county seat, is a good location, laid out for convenience in business departments. Main street is beautifully ornamented by rows of cherry trees on each side of the street There are dry goods and grocery stores, hotels. law and medical offices, work-shops, school buildings, churches and fine family residences. The merchants are Major Edward Fostor, McNeil, Wm. Transon.

Foster & Neal are manufacturers of flour; Felix Barr, mechanic; Captain Joseph Todd, Pell, G. L. Park, Blackburn, R. H. McNeill, George Bower and Davis, are lawyers. The doctors are J. B. Roberts Wiley Colvard and Manly Blevins. County Clerk, Sidney Eller; county Register, D. A. Orsborn. Resident ministers, Revs. William M. Robbins and Allen Jones. Superintendent of Sunday school, John Neal.

The population of Jefferson is made up of active, enterprising business people of moral excellence. The churches are Methodist and Presbyterian. In giving a statement of the population of Ashe county from its earlier settlements to the present time we can give only a partial list of prominent persons and families, many whose honorable, useful lives will doubtless be left out, but it is intended to give a correct account of those who, when this highly favored land was a wild indian country, periled their lives through privations, dangers, hardships and toil. opened the way to happy homes, fruitful fields, good society in a chris-tian land of schools and churches.

Henry Poe, Martin Gambill, Thomas Sutherland, Timothy Perkins, Captain John Cox, Henry Hardin, Canada Richardson,

James, Douglas, Daniel Dickerson, brothers, and Elijah Callaway were men of steady habits who did much for the good of society, and the fruits of their labors are enjoyed by those who live afterwards. At a later date just as worthy citizens were William Gambill—whose wife was Cynthia Cox, daughter of Captain John Cox, Sr.,— Nicholas Gentry, James Baker and Elijah Callaway. The latter was a soldier at Norfolk, Va , in the war of 1812, and represented his county in the legislature six sessions and his district in the senate five sessions. We failed to learn the name of his wife. They raised a family worthy their parents. Dr. James Callaway, of Wilkes county, was their son.

Col. George Bower was a native of Ashe county, a merchant, farmer, live-stock raiser and hotelist at Jefferson. He married a Miss Bryant the first time and Miss America Rosseau the second time. He was state senator, was elector on the ticket that elected General Andrew Jackson President both terms. Other citizens were Colonel Andrew McMillan, Absalom Bower, James and Theodore Woodie and Stephen Thomas. The latter's wife was a Miss Perkins, daughter of Timothy Perkins. Edward Weaver and Meredith Balou were iron manufacturers. Zachariah Baker's wife was Zylpia Dickson. The wife of Joshua Baker, Sheriff, was also a Miss Dickson. Frederick Severt was a worthy citizen, Matthew Carson was a representative in the State Legislature, Edward Bartlett was Sheriff and County Clerk, John M. Carson was Sheriff and merchant, Jesse Bledsoe was representative in the Legislature, and Edward Foster was a member of the convention and representative in the Legislature.

Andrew Dickson's name carries the profound respect of the community with it. Mr. Dickson is one of the oldest men now living in the county. His wife was Miss Mary McMillan, a worthy lady. They have raised a family that honored parents and country. Hon. Marshall Dickson was a respected soldier in the Confederate army, Sheriff, Clerk of the Superior court of his county and representative in the State Legislature. He married Miss Juda Halsey, an amiable good woman.

John Koontz, who married Miss Cornelia Colvard, an estimable and worthy christian lady, was the son of Rev. Jacob Koontz, whose wife was a Miss Ray. Mr. Koontz was an humble minister of the gospel in the Baptist church, a good neighbor and an upright man.

Alexander Dickson, Jesse B. McMillan, and Alexander McMillan. Jr., are worthy citizens and have excellent families. Captain Andrew McMillan, a citizen of Nathan's Creek, who commanded a company in the Confederate army, is a true friend to his country. His wife was a Miss Reeves, a good christian lady. She has gone to a happy home in the better land. Joshua Cox, grandson of Captain John Cox, of Revolutionary renown, lives in this neighborhood and is an old man. He has been twice married and raised two families. He is a respected, worthy gentleman.

Jesse Reeves, Sr., was one of the early settlers of the county. He lived on New River at the mouth of Peak Creek, about eight miles east of Jefferson. The location was first made by old Mr. Dick. He was twice married; first, to a Miss Terrell, second, Miss Mary Bower. He was a successful farmer and respected citizen. His sleeping dust rests besides that of his beloved wife, Mary, in the family graveyard.

Levi Gentry married Miss Nancy Plummer, an excellent woman, whose christian life was an ornament to home and community. Mr. Gentry was one of the county's best citizens, a practical farmer and good neighbor.

Mr. Gentry, wife, son, Andrew, and daughters, Sarah and Amanda, were members of the Methodist church. Their three sons entered the Confederate army. It is worthy of note that the Gentry family have been distinguished for their principles and patriotic love of constitutional liberty and justice. These young men of moral worth left the endearments of home and friends under a sense of duty and laid their lives on their country's altar. Their names were Andrew, Joseph and Levi. It was a source of deep sorrow when the news came of their death. Levi was a mere youth, a good boy, and loved by all who knew him. These brothers were regarded by the entire community as young men of bright character and future promise. Andrew Gentry left an excellent wife and children to mourn the loss of a good husband and kind father.

Colonel Andrew McMillan's residence was on Nathan's Creek. He married a Miss Fields, a most excellent woman. He was a good, upright citizen and raised an honorable family. He married the second time the widow Justice. Several of the family have been described on preceding pages.

DR. B. E. REEVES.

Dr. B. E. Reeves, son of Andrew and Mahala Reeves, was born at Lamar, Ashe county, N. C., on September 21st, 1866, was educated in the common schools of the country, studied medicine and graduated in the Baltimore College of Medicine and Surgery, April 14th, 1891. He has been actively employed since that time in the practice of his professsion, and from untiring patience genial kindness and success in practice made himself a most popular physician. He married Miss Pauline Welborne, a lady of talents education and refinement, such as light up happy homes and cheer the Doctor in the arduous toils of his profession. Dr. Reeves, in the true spirit of patriotism, has taken a deep interest in advocating the principles and defending the purity of liberty and justice as set forth in the Declaration of Indepence and Constitution of the United States, the grandest superstructure of civil government ever devised and established by the wisdom and genius of man He is chairman of the Gen. Democratic executive committee. He was elected to the legislature in 1898, and was chairman of the committee on public health in the historic legislature of 1899. The connty needs and has to depend on such men as Dr. Reeves to preserve the

THE SANDS OF TIME. 113

priceless heritage of our foreparents, and illustrious founders of the government at the cost of life and treasure. May future generations perpetuate their memory, follow their example, cherish their principles of opposition to tyranny and oppression, and love of home and country.

Edward and William Weaver were honored citizens who had worthy families Rev. Hiram and Elihu Weaver were local preachers in the Methodist church South. Their labors will remain bright and bear fruit long after they have laid down their silver trumpets and gone to reap their reward in heaven Rev. Dr. James Wagg was a faithful minister of the gospel in the Methodist church and a successful physician. He raised a family noted for intelligence and moral worth. Their son, Rev. Eugene Wagg, is a member of Western North Carolina Conference, filling stations and P. E , and an able minister of the gospel. Another son, Rev. John Wagg, was a fluent speaker and pulpit orator. Another son, Dr. Alfred Wagg, is a good citizen and well qualified physician. Captain Samuel Wagg, their brother, commanded a company from Ashe county in the Confederate army, a brave and chivalrous officer who was devoted to duty and kind to his company. He fell in the battle at Gettysburg—that field of carnage where such men as Captain Wagg, Col. Sidney Stokes, Gen. James B. Gordon and private, patriotic, country-loving soldiers fell, and where Gen. Petigrew was killed while bringing out the shattered army. Such men's names and noble deeds are worthy to be placed on the golden pages of history and retained in memory on living hearts.

Rev. James Weaver, son of preacher Hiram Weaver, is a member of the Western North Carolina Conference, an eloquent pulpit orator, has been Presiding Elder and is now stationed in Salisbury. These useful ministers of the gospel, laboring to cultivate Immanuel's land, and establish the peaceful kingdom of Christ on earth for the glory of God and salvation of souls, are natives of Ashe county. Jefferson has two resident ministers. Rev. William M. Robbins, member of the Western North Carolina Conference, whose zeal and untiring devotion to his ministerial work has endeared him to his people. Rev. Allen Jones, a Presbyterian minister, stationed at Jefferson, is a popular literary teacher and an active laborer in the ministry. Rev. Ernest Gillespie is synodical superintendent of missions for the state of North Carolina. Rev. Wm. A. Murry is a Presbyterian Evangelist. These gentlemen are well qualified ministers of the gospel, whose faithful labors are accomplishing much toward building up the Redeemer's kingdom on earth.

Major Ed. Fostor, merchant and manufacturer of leather; McNeil and Transou are dealers in dry goods and groceries, Colyard, Roberts and Blevins are successful physicians; Felix Barr and Elzy Brown are good mechanics; Sidney Eller, Clerk; D. A. Orsborne, Register; Gaither McNeil, Sheriff; two church edifices and parsonages, telephone office. and two hotels. The Mountain hotel, where every accomodation that the heart could desire, with cheerful attention, from Martin Hardin, the gentlemanly proprietor, his excellent lady and her accomplished sister. The fine steel roller flour mill of this place is an important benefit to the surrounding country. The splendid meadows, green pasture fields, of luxurious growths of grass, makes Ashe county one of the leading, if not first, counties in the State for raising live stock. The abundant fruits in great varieties, its crystal streams of pure, cold water and salubrious atmosphere, make Ashe county one of the favored parts of the earth for happy homes.

Nicholas Gentry was a resident of Ashe county. His farm and home were on Nathan's Creek. He and his praiseworthy wife raised a family of intelligent, enterprising children, who have added much to the welfare and good of society. Their daughter, Mary, married James Richardson, a worthy citizen of Cranberry. Elizabeth married James Smith, Sallie married William Turner, James Gentry married Miss Mary Smith, a very quiet, good woman, and lived on New River, eight miles east of Jefferson. They had two sons, Nicholas and Richard, noble, moral, good young men. They both fell in the Confederate army. Their untimely death was a sad loss to their family. Hon. Richard Gentry married a Miss Harboard, an amiable lady. His residence was at Old Field, in the southern part of the county. Mr. Gentry was a man of great energy, a systematic farmer, minister of the gospel in the Baptist church, and employed his superior talents not only in preaching the gospel, but in warmly advocating the cause of temperance. He filled the office of Justice of the Peace, was representative in both branches of the legislature and was Clerk of the super-

rior court of Ashe county for many years.
Taken all together, he was a remarkable man,
combining so many qualifications for useful
employment for the good of society. It is
fortunate for any community that such men
employ their time and talents for the good of
their country, when they live and labor among
them.

Aquilla Greer came from Franklin county,
Va., at an early day and settled on Grassy
Creek, in the northern part of the county He
was an enterprising business man, and fitted
up one of the nicest farms in the county. He
married a Miss Fielder, of Elk Creek, Va.
They had one son and two daughters. One
of their daughters married Ephraim Gentry,
a worthy citizen who lived in Grayson county,
near New River, six or seven miles south east
of Independence. Another daughter married
Elias Draughn. His son, John F. Greer was
an upright, persevering man. He married a
Miss Jones, of Caldwell county, N. C. He
was a successful farmer, live-stock dealer and
for many years conducted successfully a
large mercantile business, and perhaps sold
more general merchandise than any one store
keeper who did business in the county, giving
general satisfaction to his large number of

customers. Esqire Greer's son's were determined, energetic business men. Cartlett Greer and his brother, John, were highly respected good soldiers in the Confederate army. The two men and their brother, Jones Greer, have passed away from the active business of life. Calvin Greer, their only brother now living, is one of Grassy Creek's best citizens. He married Miss Mary Pierce, a daughter of Rufus and Elizabeth Pierce, a charming good woman. Mr. Greer is a successful farmer, producer and is a dealer in fine cattle and other live stock. They have an excellent family of much moral worth.

Martin Gambill, who married a Miss Nall, was one of the first settlers of the county on New River, in the eastern part. He was a true patriot in the days of the Revolution. Colonel Ben Cleveland sent a letter to him by a messenger to carry to Colonel William Campbell. He went to Enoch Orsborne, who lived on New River, near the mouth of Bridle Creek, Va., to borrow a horse. Esq. Enoch Orsborne took the harness off of his horse, where he was plowing, and loaned to him to ride to Washington county, Virginia. Col. Campbell, in compliance with the request, came wih three hundred and fifty men and

joined Cleveland, McDowell, Lenoir and others
to meet Col. Ferguson, the British command
er of English and Tories. Mr. Martin Gambill died soon after the war His amiable widow lived to a great age, loved, honored and
respected William Gambill and his worthy
lady lived and died on the same farm. Their
son, Esquire James Gambill, married Miss
Lucy Reeves, of Virginia Esquire Gambill,
after living a useful citizen. good neighbor and
worthy christian, passed over to the shore of
immortality, leaving his faithful good wife a
widow. Their son, Preston, is also a good
citizen, living in the same neighborhood. He
married Miss Bettie Colvard, daughter of William and Sallie Colvard, who adorns her home
as a cheerful good wife and mother.

Esquire Rufus Pierce lived on south fork
of New River a short distance east of Chest
nut Hill. He married Miss Elizabeth Scott,
of Smith county, Virginia. She possessed
the enobling virtues of true womanhood and a
true spirit of Christian kindness. She was a
loving light in a happy home. Esquire Pierce
was a stay in his neighborhood, to sustain
civil government, and a pillow to the church.
Their example for industry and economy in
providing well for the temporal comforts of

life, and the part they took in the cause of true christian religion, is an example that cannot die. St. Paul said in his letter to the Hebrews: "By faith Abel offered unto God a more excellent sacrifice than Cain, by which he obtained witness that he was righteous. God testifying of his gifts, and by it he being dead yet speaketh."

Esquire Stephen Thomas, a native of Grayson county. Va . was for many years a worthy citizen of Ashe county, at Creston, was an extensive farmer. Justice of the Peace, merchant and live-stock raiser. He married a Miss Perkins, the daughter of Timothy Perkins, one of the pioneer settlers of Grayson county, Virginia, an intelligent, pious, christian lady. Their family of children were distinguished for moral worth, diligence in business and devotion to religion This pious family did much for the establishment of order and good society. David Worth married their daughter and settled at the same place, was for several years a successful merchant, Justice of the Peace and member of the special quarterly term of county court. Col. George W. Reeves also married one of their daughters, Miss Caroline. Wiley Reeves, for many years a merchant at Jefferson, was their son, an esteemed citizen. He married a Miss Horton, an excellent lady.

Thomas Sutherland was an early settler, on the north fork of New River in the western part of the couuty. His wife's name is unknown to us. Mr. Sutherland was an energetic business man, farmer and live-stock producer. Their sons were Alfred, Joseph, Reuben and Thomas. They were men of intelligence and business qualifications. Their lineal descendants have been noted for their talents and morality. Rev. Alexander C. Sutherland, of Carroll county, Va., is a grandson of Thomas Sutherland. Sr., and Rev. Roby Sutherland, great-grandson. although quite a young man, is distinguished as a pulpit orator and stationed at Bristol, Tenn.

Zechariah Baker was one of Ashe county's best citizens, a farmer, and representative in the legislature. He married Miss Zylphia Dickson, a good woman, affectionate mother, faithful wife and kind neighbor. John Baker, their son, lives near Dresden, north fork of New River. He married a Miss Eller, a lady possessed of enobling virtues. Mr. Baker is a successful farmer and live-stock raiser. He has served his county as Sheriff for several years in honor to himself and satisfaction to his people. Rev. Joseph King married his daughter, a worthy lady. He was a faithful local Methodist preacher. He died in the prime of life, leaving an example that is a blessing to the community.

John Gentry is an industrious farmer and kind neighbor. He married Miss Mary Reeves, daughter of Alexander and Lydia Reeves. She is a worthy lady, faithful wife, kind mother and good neighbor, They have raised an intelligent family of children.

Charles Reeves, the son of Mary and Jesse Reeves, was born, raised and lived on the old homestead. He married Miss Mary McMillan, a good woman, faithful and industrious wife and mother who has taken much interest in the welfare, success and happiness of her family. Charles Reeves was an upright, honest, good man—a purer patriot never lived—a respected and honored Confederate Soldier. He died sometime ago, leaving a widow and large family of children. Peace to his honored rest.

Sidney Transou is an honored citizen of Ashe county. He came here from Wilkes county and settled on Peak Creek. He is a systematic farmer and dealer in improved live stock. He and his sons are extensively engaged in the mercantile business. His wife was a Miss Mastin, a good christian lady. Esquire Transou and his worthy family have done much to build up the church in their neighborhood. They have erected near their family residence a neat Methodist church edifice, and have a well-conducted Sunday school.

Esquire John H. Carson married a Miss Ella Mastin, a sister of Mrs. Transou, and live on the north fork of New River near Healing Springs. They are worthy members of the Methodist church South. Esquire William Carson, his excellent wife and family, live near Bethel Methodist church, which they have, to some extent, been instrumental in building. Their daughter, Miss Martha Ellen, is a young lady of bright intelligence, a literary teacher in common schools, and an efficient Sunday school superintendent. Esq. Carson has an excellent family. Mr. John Reeves married their daughter, Miss Fannie, and Mr. Rufus Pennington married another of his daughters. Esquire Carson has three other accomplished daughters and one son who are an honor to parents and country.

Captain John Cox came from the Valley of Virginia to Montgomery county, lived there with his family for a few years. John Craig married his sister, Mary Cox, whose son, Robt. C. Craig, was a member of congress for a number of years, and for whom Craig county was named. Capt. Cox and family moved from Montgomery county to Grayson county, Va., and settled on New River, about ten miles west of Grayson Old Court House, and was living there in time of the Revolutionary war. He was a Regulator, commanding a company, and was called upon to assist in keeping order and peace. He did much to put a stop to bad conduct and Tory depradations. After the war he purchased lands at the mouth of Cranberry Creek, on New River, in Ashe county. He was an energetic business man. conducted a large farm and raised stock. He lived to a good old age. He now rests in his honored grave on the same farm. He had two sons and four daughters, Katharine, Jane, Elizabeth and Mary, James and Joshua. Joshua Cox married a Miss Richardson. Elizabeth married Thomas McGinsey. Katharine married Henry Hardin. Jane married Cannady Richardson. James married widow Terrell, and remained in Grayson county, Va. They had one son, Solomon Cox, who went to the eastern part of Kentucky, and was a leading citizen and extexsive live-stock dealer. Joshua Cox came with parents to Cranberry and married a Miss Richardson, was a farmer and raised a worthy family. Esquire William Cox married Miss Elizabeth Reeves who adorned her home with all that constitutes a good wife, kind mother and industrious house keeper. He was a nice farmer, stock-raiser and miller. They raised an enterprising, intelligent family. Two of their sons, David and Hiram, were honored soldiers in the Confederate army and were killed in battle. It is a sad comment on the misfortunes of war when the brightest and best young men immolate their lives on their country's altar in defense of its constitutional rights. Their son, Levi, was an honored soldier in the Confederate army. He married a Miss Miller, a most excellent woman—just such as make a contented husband and happy home. The lineal descendants of this worthy family are scattered through many of the Western states. Joshua Cox's, (Sr.) daughter married William Mulky, an enterprising and well to-do citizen of Indiana. Their son, Samuel Cox, was an industrious, persevering, quiet citizen. He married Miss Mary Long, daughter of John and Susan Long, one of earth's purest and best women, who did her part well in all the endearing relations of life. Their oldest son was a promising young man, apt scholar, remarkable mechanical genius and a good moral character with the promise of a bright future, while returning from preaching one Sabbath evening, was killed by lightning conducted by the metalic poin of an umbrella he was holding while a heavy shower of rain was falling.

Solomon V. Cox, son of Samuel and Mary Cox, living seven miles east of Jefferson, is an extensive farmer, noted for his active, energetic perseverance in business. He was a respected and honored soldier in the Confederate army. Solomon V. Cox married Miss Mary Jane Cox, daughter of Dr. Aras B. and Phebe E. Cox. An obituary published in The Alleghany Star, August, 24th, 1899, reads:

"Mary Jane Cox was born January, 13th, 1846, and was carried by angel waiters to the home of the soul, August 7th, 1899, age 53 years, six months and twenty-four days. Her parents sent her to Lenoir Female College where she obtained a liberal education As a school girl she was obedient and docile. In 1868 she was happily married to S. V. Cox, which union was blessed with seven children, six girls and one boy, two of whom preceeded her to the better world. At the early age of eight years she gave her heart to God and joined the Methodist Episcopal church South, in which she remained a faithful and consistent member until the Lord said 'It is enough come up higher.' She loved her church, both in doctrine and discipline, and was a liberal contributor to its support. Whatever her church asked of her she endeavored to do. She was always anxious for the appointment, whatever it might be, to be placed in full and it was usually done. She loved her preachers, and alwas gave the very best she had. Her home was the preacher's home. Oh, how much she will be missed. But while she loved her church and its ministry, she was far from being bigoted and narrow in her views toward other denominations. She always entertained a pleasant feeling and had a kind word for her sister churches, and lent a helping hand to every movement that had for its object the glory of God and the betterment of humanity. She loved and took an active part in Sunday school work, filling, at times, the office of superintendent. One of the last things that she talked about was the Sunday school, and gave her daughter, Mrs. Hart, money with which to purchase literature for the Sunday school. Sister Cox was an excellent business woman. Her husband's business was such that it kept him from home much of the time, consequently the cares and responsibilities of the home life devolved upon her, which she managed with great skill and adaptability. She possessed the happy fac-

ulty of making friends and gaining the esteem
of her neighbors. Her heighbors are her
greatest eulogists. Those who knew her best
loved her most. She was no respector of persons; she treated the rich and the poor alike.
She never turned a needy one empty from her
door. She loved her neighbors and assisted
them in sickness, comforted them in sorrow
and when they were in want administered un-
them. This noble woman is gone. We laid
her to rest in the cemetery at Senter church
while surrounded by a large assembly of loved
ones, to await the resurrection morn. She
leaves an aged father, a devoted husband, five
affectionate children, two brothers in the far
West, and a large circle of friends to mourn
their loss. WM. M. ROBBINS,
"Her Pastor."

David Cox, brother of William and Samuel Cox, married a Miss Jones and moved to
Indiana. These two large families and their
lineal descendants are scattered through the
Western states.

There are several villages in Ashe county.
Healing Springs, with fine bromide mineral
water, a splendid place for a summer resort,
for health and comfort, with all necessary
buildings for families, and boarding-house
entertainments. Creston, on the north fork
of New River, is a pleasant place, with stores
and family residences. Laurel Springs is an

active place of business—a trading point—and has a school building and churches. Liberty Hill and Bellview academies are in the eastern part of the county.

There are rich deposits of magnetic and othe iron ores, copper and other specimens of metal.

Captain John Dent is one of the best citizens, systematic farmer and live-stock raisers living a few miles east of Jefferson. He married a Miss Sanders, of Virginia, a worthy christian lady and a devoted member of the M. E. church. Captain Dent is also one of the best informed men, in the knowledge of minerals and modes of operating and working them, in the county or state. The advancement of all that pertains to temporal and spiritual interests is very gratifying and gives psomise to Ashe county's worthy people of a bright future.

There are many—very many—good people for whom we entertain the highest respect, whose worthy and faithful lives are worthy of entry on the pages of history, but we have not the space within the limit of this history.

The author of these sketches is thankful to a kind Providence for a home twenty-four years in Alleghany and Ashe counties, from

1845 to 1869, and the associations with the good people of this country.

May the providence of an all-wise, infinite loving Father in heaven preserve the county in peace, prosperity and happiness for ages to come.

CHAPTER VIII.

NORTH-WESTERN NORTH CAROLINA.

Surry County.

Surry county was formed in 1790 from Rowan county which, until said date, comprehended a large portion of Western North Carolina, from beyond the Yadkin to the Missippi river. Its name is Saxon, and signifies the Soutn River. Surry county is situated in the north-western portion of North Carolina. It is bounded on the north by the Virginia line, east by Stokes county, south by Yadkin, and west by Wilkes and Ashe.

Its capital was Rockford. Population in 1880 was 15,294. The patriotism of the women of this region deserves a perpetual record. It was their heroic conduct that inspired their husbands in the cause of liberty. They urged the men to leave home, and prefer to die than be slaves, while they stayed at home and worked with their own hands at the plow and with the hoe, by day, to provide sustenance for their families, and at night with the spinning-wheel and loom, they made the clothing.

In this county is the celebrated Ararat. or Pilot Mountain. It rises gradually to the height of several hundred feet, and terminates in a flat surface From its summit is a noble view of the surrounding country. The productions of Sury county are wheat, rye, corn, oats, cotton, potatoes and tobacco. The first county capital has been changed from Rockford to Dobson, named in honor of William P. Dobson, a distinguished citizen, state-man and representative. Mt. Airy and Pilot Mountain are prosperous villages in the county, each containiug several hundred population of active, enterprising business people. Rev. Kelly Boyer, a member of Western North Carolina Conference. M. E. church South, is stationed at Mt. Airy and is an able, faithful minister of the gospel.

Tyre Glen was a citizen of Surry county, a man whose industry and economy was not often equalled and never surpassed. He acquired much wealth and was an honor to his county. William P. Dobson and worthy family resided in Surry. His wife was an amiable and refined lady. Their son, Joseph Dobson, was a lawyer of fine talent, an honored member of the bar, was representative in both branches of the legislature, a true patriot and a wise statesman. Col. Joseph Williams settled in this county before the Revolutionary war. He was distinguished for his enterprise, activity and patriotism. He died at a good old age, loved and respected by all who knew him. He married Mis Lanier, a woman of strong mind and exemplary virtues. From this marriage sprang Gen. Robt. Williams, a man of distinguished attainments and great research; John Williams, distinguished in Tennessee at the battle of Horse Shoe between Gen. Jackson and the Creek Indians—a long and desperate battle. He married a sister of Hugh Lawson White. He died leaving a son Joseph, whose daughter married Hon. R. M. Pierson, one of North Carolina's supreme court judges. Lewis Williams is well known in history as a patriot and statesman. He was a member in the House of Commons, elected a member of congress in 1815, served continuously until 1842. He died in congress,

Feb. 23rd, 1842. There are others of the Williams family equally distinguished as men of talent and patriotism, who held high offices in honor to themselves and satisfaction to their people.

Jesse Franklin was of Surry county. He was distinguished for his sincere patriotism. sound sense and unassuming deportment. In 1794 he was elected a member of the House of Commons; in 1775 a member of congress; in 1799 state senator from Surry; United States senate 1807-1813. In 1820 he succeeded John Branch as Governor. This long career as a public servant is evidence of his personal worth and popularity.

Judge J. F. Graves was the grandson of Hon. Jesse Franklin, and was distinguished for his sound judgement, moral worth and patriotic love of country. He was an honored soldier in the Confederate army, Judge of the second district superior court, died honored and respected as one of North Carolina's noblest men.

James R. Dodge was a successful lawyer and Clerk of the supreme court. He married a Miss Williams and raised and educated a worthy family of children.

Gideon Bryan was a resident of Surry

county, an earnest, upright citizen. He and his family honored their county. Richard Gwyn, of Elkin, was notable as a man of business, his piety and devotion to religion and the advancement of Christ's kingdom on earth.

Surry county may well be proud of her past record and cherish bright hopes for the future.

CHAPTER IX.

NORTH-WESTERN NORTH CAROLINA.

WATAUGA COUNTY.

Watauga county was formed in 1849 from Ashe, Caldwell, Wilkes and Yancy. It derives its name from the river that runs through it, an Indian name, which signifies River of Islands. It is situated in the extreme north western part of the state, and is bounded on the north by Ashe county, east by Wilkes, south by Yancey and McDowell, west by the Yellow mountains, which separates it from Tennessee.

Boone is the capital, named in honor of the celebrated Daniel Boone, who once lived near Holman's Ford, on the Yadkin river, about eight miles from Wilkesboro. Col. Boone had for a time a camp in this county, also one in

Ashe, on Horse creek. The south fork of New river runs through this county.

The scenery is beautiful; fine forest of timber, towering mountains, green valleys, crystal streams of pure cold water, lawns, shade trees, flowers, and fine orchards.

The productions are wheat, corn, rye, oats, buckwheat and potatoes. The variety of grasses make this a fine grazing section.

Boone, the county capital, is beautifully situated, carefully laid out for convenience in business departments. The advantages of water power are many. It contains valuable minerals in iron and copper.

It was here in North Carolina that Boone was raised; here his youthful days were spent, and here that bold spirit was trained which so fearlessly encountered the perils through which he passed in after life. His fame is a part of her property, and she has inscribed his name on a town where his youth was spent.

Connected with this county's history is the name of Gen. James Sevier. He did much toward defending the people from Indian depradations and violence. He possessed the qualifications of citizen, soldier, statesman and patriot. Such men deserve a conspicuous place in history. Gen Sevier was commissioned captain by Governor Dunmore, of Virginia, and fought in the battle of Point Pleasant. He came with an exploring party to the Holston river, east Tennessee, then (1769) a part of North Carolina, and directed the construction of the first fort on the Watauga river. While defending the fort he discovered a young lady, tall and erect, coming towards the fort pursued by Indians, who counted on her capture as they passed between her and the gate, but turning suddenly she eluded her pursuers, leaped the palisades and fell into the arms of Capt. John Sevier. This remarkable, active and resolute woman wass Miss Katharine Sherrill, who became the wife of the Colonel and the bosom friend of the General, the Governor, the people's patriotic friend, John Sevier, and the mother of ten children, who could rise up and call her blessed. Their son, Rev. Elbert Sevier, was a distinguished minister of the gospel and a member of the Holston Annual conference, for many years in charge of circuit stations, and Presiding Elder

The history of Watauga from its early settlement reflects honor on its population. They occupied a position exposed to Indian depredation on one side and Tories on the other.

Many distinguished families have lived in Watauga and some still live there. Among the number are Hortons, Greens, Counsels, Hardins, Farthings, Masts and Binghams. Hon. Nathan Horton was a representative in the legislature in 1800, state senate 1805-6. James Horton was a member of the legislature in 1834, and Jonathan Horton was also a representative in the legislature, Noah Mast and Reuben Mast were representatives in the legislature.

John Hardin was the son of Henry Hardin, one of the early settlers of the county. He married Miss Katharine Cox, daughter of Captain John Cox, of Revolutionary fame. Henry Hardin and excellent wife lived to a good old age.

The Horton family were noted for their love of country and were ever ready to defend it in the hour of necessity. The Masts were early settlers of Watauga, firm in principle, and true to their country's welfare.

There were four Farthing brothers, ministers of the gospel in the Baptist church, whose lives and labors in the cause of salvation as a band of earthly brothers and brothers in the spiritual kingdom of the world's

Redeemer, battled against the powers of darkness and held up the standard of the cross of Christ in love and power. These good brothers' names and useful lives are worthy a place on the pages of history. Jordan Councill was a worthy citizen, and married a Miss Bower, and raised a family that honored parents and country. William B. Councill was a successful physician. James was a member of the State convention. Miss Bettie Councill was the devoted wife of Colonel George Folk, who endeared himself, not only to the people of his county, but State, for the interest he took and services rendered for his country. He was a worthy, good man, and true patriot.

Judge Green was a native of Watauga, a man of talents, and distinguished himself as an able judge of law, giving general satisfaction where he held courts throughout the State. Mr. Allen Green and family are worthy residents of the county. Mr. Bingham was the first clerk of the superior court of Watauga county.

Spencer Blackburn is a native of Watauga a young man of talents, who has made quite a reputation as a successful lawyer, and is associated with Mr. Councill, of the same county, in the practice of law, and has an office at

Jefferson. Welborn Hardin, son of Henry and Katharine Hardin, was one of the county's best cititizens. He married Miss ———————. Martin Hardin, hotel keeper at Jefferson, is their son, also William Hardin, of Sparta, Alleghany county, now deceased.

There are several objects of natural scenery attached to Watauga county. The Blowing Rock, in the southern part of the county. Fine preparation is made to entertain visitors seeking a place of health resort, where pure water, salubrious air, and delightful scenery, lend to the place a power of attraction seldom equaled or excelled. The Grandfather mountain, in the south western part of the county, rises in sublime grandeur, a great giant, standing amidst the floating clouds, bidding defiance to storms—a monument to the works of nature's God. There are a number of places of note which the limits of this work will not give room to publish. Valle Cruisie, some miles west of Boone, where a college was commenced and abandoned, is one of the many places of intetest.

May succeeding generations look back and honor ancestors and enjoy peace, prosperity and happiness.

CHAPTER X.

NORTH-WESTERN NORTH CAROLINA.

WILKES COUNTY.

Wilkes county was formed in the year 1777, from Surry, and called in honor of John Wilkes, an English statesman. It is situated in the extreme north-west portion of the state. It is bounded on the north by the Blue Ridge, which separates it from Ashe county, east by Surry, south by Alexander, west by Ashe and Watauga counties.

Wilkesboro, the capital, is well situated, conveniently arranged into business departments. The productions are corn, wheat, rye, oats, potatoes, sorgum cane, tobacco, wool and cotton.

The beautiful range of Bushy mountains on the south and towering heights of the Blue

Ridge on the north, make a scene of almost unrivaled grandeur. Along the river and its tributary streams the richest lands, yielding both cereals and vegetables, and fine groves of timber, oak, poplar, and pine, are found. At but few places in all this country can be found finer farming lands than the widespread bottoms on the Yadkin river.

Montford Stokes, long a resident of this county, was born about 1760. He entered the Revolutionary army, was taken prisoner, near Norfolk, and for seven months confined on a prison-ship. For a number of years he was Clerk of Rowan superior circuit, and clerk of the senate, where he enjoyed such popularity as to be elected senator in congress two terms. He served several sessions in the state legislature, in 1826 and 1829 was a member of the House of Commons, and again in 1830, when he was elected Governor of the state. He was appointed by Gen. Jackson Indian agent in Arkansas, where he removed and lived until his death, in 1842. Gov. Stokes married Mary, the daughter of Col. Henry Irwin, of Edgecome. This union was blessed with several children. He was Major of the North Carolina regiment in the late war with Mexico.

Col. Benjamin Cleveland, the hero of

King's mountain, and after whom Cleveland county is called, was a brave and meritorious officer, and was the hero of many fights with the Tories.

General William Lenoir resided in Wilkes county. His life, character and services have been recorded by an able and familiar hand. The following is extracted from the Raleigh Register, June 22nd, 1839, and recorded in Wheeler's history of North Carolina, from which the following is taken:

"This venerable patriot and soldier died at his residence at Fort Defiance in Wilkes county, on Monday, May 6th, 1839, aged 88 years."

Gen Lenoir was born in Brunswick, county, Va., on the 20th of May, 1751, O. S., and descended from poor but respectable French ancestry. When about eight years old his father removed to Tar river, near Tarboro, N. C., where he resided until his death, which happened shortly after. He received no other education than such as his own personal exertions permitted him to acquire When about 20 years of age he married Miss Ballard, a lady possessing those domestic and heroic virtues which qualified her for sustaining the privations and hardship of frontier life, which it

THE SANDS OF TIME. 145

was her destiny afterwards to encounter. In 1775 Gen. Lenoir removed his family to the county of Wilkes.

Col. Findley and Col. Gordon were early settlers of Wilkes. They deserve the highest praise. James Gwyn was a resident of Wilkes, owned and systematically cultivated a large farm on Yadkin river. He was a good citizen and raised a family whose piety and devotion to christianity will leave fruits to ripen in eternity.

John Alexander lived on Roaring river, near the Blue Ridge, and was a good citizen. His wife was a Miss Thompson, of Alleghany county. They raised a worthy family. Shuby Luncford, of Ashe county, married their daughter. Miss Nancy Alexander. Mr. Holbrook married Miss Fannie Alexander, another of their daughters

Hon. John Q. A. Bryan resides at Trap Hill. He was a member of the convention to amend the constitution of North Carolina. He served as an officer in the Union army during the unfortunate war between the states. Col. William Barber, of Wilkes, a meritorious officer, fell in the Confederate army—sacrificed his life for the love of liberty and justice. Peace to his sleeping dust.

The Chronicle is edited by Robt. Deal, and published at Wilkesboro. It is a bold and fearless advocate of the principles it believes to be right. The Curfew, published at Absher, is a neat little family paper. Mr. Sawyer is publisher.

Dr. George Doughton, of North Wilkesboro, is a successful physician and owner and proprietor of a good drug store. Rev. Mr. Robinson, a Presbyterian minister is stationed in North Wilkesboro, and has served the people faithfully for a number of years.

The location of the railroad on the north side of the Yadkin river, opposite Wilkesboro, has built an addition to the town, known as North Wilkesboro, an active place of business.

Dr. James Callaway, an eminent physician and statesman, resided a number of years in Wilkesboro. His first wife was a Miss Carmichael, and his second wife was Miss Ann Eacles. They raised a family of intelligent, enterprising children.

General. James B. Gordon was a pure patriot who loved his country and his country loved him. He commanded a brigade in the Confederate army, was there wounded and died, an honor to his country.

Col. Sidney Stokes was educated at West

Point. He was Maj. of the North Carolina regiment in the war with Mexico, and commanded a regiment in the Confederate army.

The Whitingtons, Abshers and Colyards were leading families and worthy citizens of the county. Uncle Isaiah McGrady—as he was usually called—lived at the foot of the Blue Ridge, near Mulberry Gap. He and his worthy family were an honor to their country and were loved and respected.

Wilkes county has a proud record and a bright future.

CHAPTER XI.

NORTH-WESTERN NORTH CAROLINA.

Battle of King's Mountain.

One of the most important events recorded in modern history was the victory gained at the battle of King's mountain.

Cornwallis, commander-in-chief of the British army, expecting the conquest of North Carolina to follow the recovery of South Carolina, spread his troops to repress patriotic movements, and quickened Tory zeal on the left wing of his army, with Col. Furguson, an officer with great energy and courage, in command of a large force marching toward the Alleghanies.

News of their movements was received in north-western North Carolina and south-western Virginia. Cols. Benjamin Cleveland,

John Sevier, Isaac Shelby, Wm. Campbell, Mc-Dowell, Wm. Lenoir assembled the militia from the valleys of the Yadkin, Holston, Clinch and New river, each commanding their respective regiments.

The country had to rely mainly for its defense on the skill and military genius of brave commanders and the valor, firmness and integrity of the militia which had to get in readiness in quick time. The honesty of purpose, the appreciation of homes, the love of families, welfare of the community, the freedom from oppressive laws, the enjoyment and possession of the blessings and happiness of inherited rights, will ever remain as garlands crowning officers and soldiers.

These gallant officers and men assembled in readiness to march. Col Campbell was placed in command. After a rapid march they met the enemy. Col. Ferguson had taken position on King's mountain, near the line dividing North and South Carolina. He stated he had taken a position from which the Almighty could not drive him. In order to take the British command by surprise, and before Colonel Ferguson could be reinforced, Colonel Campbell and his brave home-defenders sat in their saddles thirty hours, with but few minutes intermission. Arriving at the foot of the mountain at day-light on the morning of October 7th, 1780, they dismounted and marched up the mountain, after a fierce conflict, being repulsed three times. Colonel Ferguson made a daring attempt to break through the lines and was slain. One hundred and fifty of his bravest and best men fell before the mountaineers' unerring rifles. The survivors, eight hundred in number, surrendered. Twenty-five tories were hung. This battle was the turning point of the war. It crippled Lord Cornwallis' army, gave General Nathaniel Green time to get his command ready for action. The battle of Guilford was fought, the British army being defeated. Cornwallis surrendered to General Washington, at Little York, Va., soon after.

General Isaac Shelby was originally from Maryland, and was with his father at the battle of Point Pleasant. He was the first governor of Kentucky, in 1802, and again in 1812. General William Campbell was an officer of distinction and promise. He died young of fever, at Hanover Court House, Va , on his way to join LaFayette, before Yorktown. General John Sevier was of French descent He was in the battle of Point Pleasant. He was Governor of the transitory state of Frankland and first governor of Tennessee.

CHAPTER XII.

NORTH-WESTERN NORTH CAROLINA.

Life of the Author and His Wife

I, Aras B. Cox, was born in Floyd county, Va., January 25th, 1816. My parents owned a farm on Beaver Creek, where they enjoyed life in quietude and cheerfulness. I was educated in the common schools of the country, such as it afforded at that time. I attended school, accompanied by my elder sister, Eliza beth, when in my sixth and seventh years. William Barton, an old crippled man, was my teacher. My parents took much interest in edncating their children, as far as they were able. The love manifested, the toils endured, the continual care exercised by the kindest of parents for their family's welfare, will remain embalmed in sacred memory until the faculties of perception fades from this mortal body. I had five brothers Cloyd, Ross, Jordan, Henry and James. and two sisters, Sarah and Elizabeth. In 1824 my father sold his land and bought other land in the western part of the county. The charms of that lovely home, the large spring of clear, cold water, the surrounding hills, and nearby beautiful pine groves and fine orchard of delicious fruit, with generous, good neighbors, made life worth the living.

I began teaching school when 18 years of age—working on the farm in summer and teaching in winter, studying books at home at night. My mind was seriously impressed in early life with the importance of living religiously.

When but a boy I was working in a field when the wind blew a tree on the horse I was plowing and crushed him to the earth I narrowly escaped being crushed myself. In early life I made a trip to Indiana, going down the Ohio river on a flat boat, and was caught in a terrible storm above Cincinnati. With great difficulty the boat was saved from sinking and rowed to shore. I felt it was through a divine Providence that I still lived.

In 1841, in partnership with a cousin, Asa Bishop, bought a farm in Carroll county, Va.

We sold our possessions after making one crop.—not admiring bachelor life.

In 1841 I began reading medicine under Dr. Mark D. Stoneman, as preceptor, an able physician and esteemed friend.

In the spring of 1842 I took a sad leave of the loved home of my youth and went to Bridle Creek, Grayson county, Va. to teach school, when the early settlers of that community had established a state of society where prosperity and happiness were richly enjoyed, and the triumphs of christian religion are spreading their balmy wings over a fine church edifice, academy of learning and a prosperous people. We spent most of the time of three years here teaching and dealing in live stock, and, when an opportunity afforded, in reading and studying the science of medicine. Our stay with these good people was pleasant, and is remembered as a green plat by a crystal spring beneath a cooling shade where I rested while on life's journey.

I had, previous to this time, sought forgiveness of my sins and regenerating grace, and felt that God gave me peace and pardoned and converted my soul. I went, in company with my esteemed uncle, Rev. Henry Bishop, to New Hope church, in Montgomery county,

Va., and was received into the Methodist Episcopal church by Rev Zane Bland, preacher in charge, June. 1842, and was licensed as a local preacher, under recommendation of quarterly conference, at Hillsville, Va., by P. E Thomas K. Catlett, April 1843.

On the 23rd of February, 1845, I was married to Phebe Edwards, whose piety as a faithful, good wife, threw across life's pathway a mellow light of love and joy. We settled in Alleghany county, at that time Ashe county. My wife's father died when she was three years of age. Her widowed mother had been confined by paralysis for several years and could not walk. Our residence was near where my wife could be with her a part of the time until 1851, when Mrs. Jane Edwards, who possessed more than ordinary talents, after a life of christian precept and example, and unceasing toil in the wise management of business for the welfare of her family and friends, patiently and peacefully passed away in June, 1851, and was buried in the family graveyard by the side of her deceased husband, David Edwards, who preceded her to the grave 21 years.

In 1849 I was elected Clerk of the superior court of Ashe county, when Ashe and

Alleghany were one county, and in 1853 was reelected to tne same office.

I sold my farm in Alleghany county and bought a larger one seven miles east of Jefferson and moved there.

In 1852 my parents left Floyd county, Va., and came to live with us. Mt. Zion was our church and place of membership. In the fall of 1847 I was ordained deacon by the venerable Bishop, James O. Andrew, at Jonesboro, Tenn., and in 1847 was ordained Elder by Bishop John Early, at Marion, Smith county, Va. During all these years much of my time was actively employed in practicing medicine and surgery,

In 1861 the unfortunate war between the states spread its dark cloud over the country. The brightest, purest and best young men entered the Confederate army. I was in the service most of the war as captain and chaplain. The war was a sad calamity. The Southern people honestly believed the principles of the constitution were disregarded and their just rights denied them. But secession was not the proper source of redress. Such conflicts are enough (were such a thing possible) to make the guardian genius of American liberty shed tears of blood. Reconstruction,

Dr. Aras B. and Wife, Phebe E. Cox.

THE SANDS OF TIME. 157

in many things, did the Southern states great injustice. We suffered a pecuniary loss, the fruits of years of toil and hard labor, from which we never fully recovered.

In the fall of 1869 we moved to Hamburg, Iowa, where I had an extensive practice in medicine, part of the time associated with Dr. Thomas H. Bragg, a graduate of Rush Medical college, of Chicago. He was a worthy christian gentleman. Here, with the help of my son Charles, I farmed for some years.

Moses U. Payne, a local preacher, member of the M. E. church South, was a man of wealth and deep piety. Soon after our arrival at Hamburg Mr Payne, having much land on Mission river bottom, brought his family there to live, and assisted us in organizing the first class in the Methodist church in that part of south-western Iowa and north western Missouri—the corner of the states joining. The good people of that rich farming country helped us build in Hamburg a fine church. Rev. M. U. Payne gave $500.00 toward building the church. The church edifice cost $2,700. Dr. Miller, professor in Howard Female College, Fayetteville, Mo., preached the dedicatory sermon to a large and attentive congregation. Rev. O. Howell was our first

Presiding Elder and Rev. John S. Rooker was preacher in charge for the conference year. I traveled as a supply on the new circuit, of Rock Port, St. Joseph district Mission conference one year. During our year's service we added some new appointments, making a four weeks' circuit with fifteen preaching stations. It is pleasant to recollect our associations with the good people of that country. Granville H. Cox and worthy family moved from Virginia to Atchison county, Mo., and did much for the church. He and his good christian wife have gone to reap a rich reward in the better world.

In the spring of 1881, while we were living on Mission river bottom, in Atchison county, Mo., a great flood came and the river spread from seven to ten miles wide. We lost fencing and other property and the land washed over and partly ruined. We left there in 1882 and moved to Madison county, Neb., sold our property there, and, in company with our three sons, Edward, Charles and Albert. moved to Blaine county, in 1885, and located homes on Buffalo Flats. In these changes of homes in different states the Lord was very good to us amid scenes of danger, sickness and death.

In the practice of medicine, traveling in extremely cold weather almost continually, chilling the blood in my eyes, produced cataract. I was totally blind from 1888 to 1891. During these three years my wife read a chapter from the Bible regularly each night, and we would have family prayer. In June Dr. Gifford, of Omaha, extracted the discolored crystaline lens from my right eye. With magnifying glasses I now can read and write. Dr. Gifford is a distinguished occulist, and one of earth's noblest and best men, whose superior genius and skill has made many hearts glad.

Our son, Edward M. Cox, and family live in Oregon. The letters from their children give evidence of christian instruction and religious influence. Dr C. B. Cox and family live in Brewster, Blaine county, Neb., and are examples of industry, economy and perseverance.

Our oldest son was born on the 18th day of December, 1847, professed religion when but a boy, was a good, quiet boy at home and at school. He was a drummer at the camp of instruction of the Confederate army, at Raleigh, when thirteen years of age. He was attending school in Alleghany county when attacked with diptheria, and, after suffering patiently for several weeks, he died on the 11th day of March, 1864.

Albert S. A. Cox, our youngest son, a student in Marion Sims' College of Medicine, St. Louis, Mo., died on the 22nd day of January, 1891. His death was a sad loss to his aged parents. He was a good boy and died in full assurance of a happy home in heaven.

Our oldest child and only daughter, Mary Jane, was born Jan. the 13th, 1864, professed religion when eight years of age, joined the Methodist church South, was one of its most faithful members, and a warm advocate of and faithful worker in Sunday school. She was happily married to Solomon V. Cox, her now bereaved husband, Oct the 9th, 1865. Her life was spent in doing good. She possessed an extraordinary capacity for business. Her unceasing toil and kind care of her family her social friendship and genial kindness to friends and neighbors will not soon be forgotten.

After suffering patiently, with great resignation, on the 7th day of August, 1899, her spirit took its flight from its earthly tenement to join loved ones, where the blessed Savior said, "I go to prepare a place for you, that where I am ye may be also."

Phebe E. Cox was born in Alleghany county, N. C., April 2nd, 1825, the daughter of David and Jane Edwards. Her father died when she was three years of age. The pious counsel of a godly mother impressed her young mind with the importance of religion, and, when but a girl, she professed religion in a camp-meeting held at Wilson camp-ground, Grayson county, Va , and joined the Methodist chrch, in which she lived a devoted member until her death.

On the 23rd day of February, 1846 she was united in marriage to Aras B. Cox and settled in Alleghany county. Our church membership was at Mt. Zion, afterwards removed to Ashe county and united in a class at a school house near where Liberty Academy now stands.

During the unfortunate war between the states she passed through many sad trials and hardships with pecuniary loss. In 1869 the family, composed of Mrs. Cox, her husband and three sons, moved to Hamburg, Iowa, leaving their only daughter, Mary Jane, wife of Solomon V. Cox, in North Carolina. In 1882 she, with husband and two sons, removed to Madison county, Neb., remaining there three years and then moved to Blaine county, Neb., and located homes on Bffalo Flats There was no church here, but the St. Louis Advocate, as she often remarked, filled the place of Southern Methodist preaching.

In October, 1892, she received a shock of paralysis and remained in feeble health until the 6th day of the following October, she was attacked with strangulated hernia. The best medical skill was called to afford relief but in vain. The sainted wife and mother, the kindhearted neighbor, and faithful member of the church lingered until Wednesday morning, the 11th day of October, 1893, when the spirit left its earthly house to assume its glorified state and to join loved ones in praise and adoration of her Savior forever.

During her suffering no words of murmur were heard. She told her husband not to weep, that they would not be separated long. She often spoke of the satisfaction it afforded her in waiting on her husband when he was blind. Her husband had donated a lot on their homestead for a cemetery, where her body rests beside that of her son, Albert, (who died while a student at Marion Sims' College of Medicine) to await the summons of the resurrection morn.

www.ingramcontent.com/pod-product-compliance
Lightning Source LLC
Chambersburg PA
CBHW020332010526
44119CB00002B/34